GREAT AMERICAN ENTREPRENEURS

Madam C.J. Walker

Entrepreneur and Self-Made Millionaire

PJ Graham

Cavendish Square
New York

Published in 2020 by Cavendish Square Publishing, LLC
243 5th Avenue, Suite 136, New York, NY 10016

First Edition

Website: cavendishsq.com

Library of Congress Cataloging-in-Publication Data

Names: Graham, P. J., 1972- author.
Title: Madam C.J. Walker : entrepreneur and self-made millionaire / PJ Graham.
Description: First Edition. | New York : Cavendish Square, [2020] | Series: Great American entrepreneurs | Audience: Grade level 9-12. | Includes bibliographical references and index.
Identifiers: LCCN 2018058453 (print) | LCCN 2019001076 (ebook) | ISBN 9781502645449 (ebook) | ISBN 9781502645432 (library bound) | ISBN 9781502645425 (pbk.)
Subjects: LCSH: Walker, C. J., Madam, 1867-1919. | African American women executives--Biography--Juvenile literature. | Cosmetics industry--United States--History--Juvenile literature. | Entrepreneurship--Juvenile literature.
Classification: LCC HD9970.5.C672 (ebook) | LCC HD9970.5.C672 W35424 1994 (print) | DDC 338.7/66855 [B] --dc23
LC record available at https://lccn.loc.gov/2018058453

Editorial Director: David McNamara
Editor: Kristen Susienka
Copy Editor: Rebecca Rohan
Associate Art Director: Alan Sliwinski
Designer: Joe Parenteau
Production Coordinator: Karol Szymczuk
Photo Research: J8 Media

The photographs in this book are used by permission and through the courtesy of: Photo credits: Cover, p. 8 Michael Ochs Archives/Getty Images; p. 4 Everett Collection Inc./AGE Fotostock; p. 7 Sean Locke Photography/Shutterstock.com; p. 13 JHU Sheridan Libraries/Gado/Getty Images; p. 16 Universal History Archive/UIG via Getty images; p. 20 Walter Oleksy/Alamy Stock Photo; p. 23 Bettmann/Getty Images; p. 24, 32, 36, 39, 62, 65, 69, 82, 103 Madam C. J. Walker Collection, Indiana Historical Society; p. 29 f11photo/Shutterstock.com; p. 41 Madam C. J. Walker Supplemental Collection, Bass Photo Co. Collection, Indiana Historical Society; p. 44 Arthur P. Bedou/Robert Abbott Sengstacke/Getty Images; p. 47 Walter Oleksy/Alamy Stock Photo; p. 50 Chicago History Museum/Getty Images; p. 55, 59 Library of Congress/Corbis/VCG/Getty Images; p. 75 Kathy Hutchins/Shutterstock.com; p. 77 Dmadeo; cropped by Beyond My Ken/Wikimedia Commons/File:VillalewaroCrop.jpg/CC BY SA 4.0; p. 78 Hulton Archive/Getty Images; p. 85 John Vachon/Library of Congress; p. 88 Kevin Winter/Getty Images; p. 91 JHU Sheridan Libraries/Gado/Getty Images; p. 92 Photo 12/UIG/Getty Images; p. 94 Nyttend/Wikimedia Commons/File:Madame Walker Theatre Center.jpg/Public Domain; p. 97 Madam Walker Family Archives/A'Lelia Bundles; p. 98 L. Cohen/WireImage for The Weinstein Company/Getty Images; p. 100 Johnny Melton/Oklahoma Historical Society/Getty Images.

Printed in the United States of America

CONTENTS

INTRODUCTION

A Dynamic Leader for Black Women

She's been called many things—the first female, black, self-made millionaire; fraudulent imitator; marketing genius; an impulsive baby; and a woman of influence. Whatever the label, Madam C.J. Walker had an unconquerable spirit that propelled her to success within the hair-care world.

More Than a Business Woman

Throughout her life, Walker did much more than succeed in business. She also overcame racism and excelled in the limited opportunities open to her in her home state of Mississippi during the post-Civil War era. Southern lawmakers passed Jim Crow laws during this time to

This photo of Madam C.J. Walker, circa 1909, shows the entrepreneur in a stylish dress of the era.

keep black people in "their place." However, Walker found her place among entrepreneurs and eventually used her skills to create a fortune for a niche industry.

Walker's greatest accomplishment and legacy stemmed from a difficult past. After losing her hair and spending two decades doing backbreaking labor, she turned to an avenue for others like her and created hair-care products for black women. Over the next several years, building up the Madam C.J. Walker Manufacturing Company, she had to convince people that her abilities were as great as her ambitions. Along the way, she lifted up other women by boosting their self-esteem or by providing them with jobs with decent earnings and helping them start their own hair salons.

Though she was often praised for her drive and marketing skill, many people opposed what she did. Some of her products, such as the Walker method or system, helped black women achieve smoother hair at a time when some black leaders believed this meant trying to act white to get ahead. Some ministers even preached against black people straightening their hair.

Walker would try to correct people's assumptions about her products, saying her emphasis was on helping black women grow hair. Many had difficulty doing so due to a lack of understanding about hygiene, stressful lives, and poor diet. "I want the great masses of my people to take a greater pride in their appearance and to give their hair proper attention," she said in 1919. "I dare say that in the next ten years it will be a rare thing to see a kinky head of hair, and it will not be straight either."[1]

As her success grew, Walker was not shy about enjoying the fruits of her labor, and her shopping trips and expensive taste were well known. If anyone doubted her interest in

During Madam Walker's lifetime, black women straightening their hair with products like hers was a socially charged issue. Today, many different natural and straightened styles are common and socially acceptable.

helping other black people, however, they only had to look at how she helped charities and at her activism. From donating to social and charity groups to using her influence to make social and legal changes for her people, she gave generously.

A Short Life of Influence

Eventually, however, her business took a toll. So many speaking engagements, travel arrangements, and workdays affected her health. Doctors tried to convince her to give up running her company, but she could never rest more than a few weeks before taking up the helm again. She was not born to rest. Even upon her deathbed, Walker spoke of wanting to live to help her people.

Madam C.J. Walker's life was rather short, but in fifty-one years, she helped change the lives of black people in the United States and established a name that history remembers.

CHAPTER ONE

From Jim Crow to the Harlem Renaissance

It's an inspiring story: a black woman born of former slaves and living in Reconstruction America becomes a self-made millionaire. Looking closer at the life of Madam C.J. Walker, as well as the opportunities that many African Americans were just starting to experience in the mid to late 1800s, it's clear just how extraordinary this woman and her accomplishments were.

A Tentative Freedom

Having been granted their freedom at the end of the Civil War, the promise of newly acquired rights tasted sweet to many African Americans, but, as would be the case for decades to come, such promises were rarely kept. This was

This 1895 photo shows men, women, and children picking a cotton crop, much like Madam C.J. Walker did in her childhood.

especially true in the South, where tensions between former slave owners, former slaves, and even poor whites and blacks frequently boiled over into discrimination, violence, and the stripping away of liberties.

The Civil War ended in 1865, with the Union winning a hard-fought battle to preserve the country and to grant every person within it freedom. The Republican Party's Reconstruction efforts started before the war ended with the creation of the Freedmen's Bureau in March 1865; however, the assassination of President Abraham Lincoln one month later left the office to Democratic vice president Andrew Johnson. A known racist, Johnson was more lenient to the South and did little to help the newly freed slaves. He gave the states back the power to govern themselves as long as they freed their slaves, swore loyalty to the Union, and paid off their war debts.

With little to stop them, Southern states took action. They quickly passed Black Codes, or laws to limit and discriminate against the freed slaves and to ensure they still did the hard labor of the South. In South Carolina, one code required blacks to pay an annual tax of $10 to $100 ($155 to $1,551 in 2018) if they were employed in any role other than a farmer or a servant. Other measures were more extreme. In 1866, white Southerners created the Ku Klux Klan, or KKK. Members of this group used violence and terror to keep black people "in their place." With all this change, some African Americans felt they might've been better off as slaves. One said: "Most all the slaves had [a] place to live, clothes to wear, and plenty to eats, and that is more than we has now."[1]

This activity in the South angered many in the Republican-controlled Congress, so they passed two bills: one to extend the life of the Freedmen's Bureau for two more years and the other to provide citizenship to anyone born in the country, thus making former slaves equal under the law. However, Johnson vetoed the bills, saying they were too expensive, limited state's rights, and did something never done by the government before: provided assistance to a specific group of people at the exclusion of others. He never regained a relationship with Congress after this, and he was impeached in 1868 as a result.

Congress seized control by passing the Reconstruction Act of 1867 over Johnson's veto. Southern states were made to accept the Fourteenth Amendment, which gave all citizens equal protection under the law. Then, Congress passed the Fifteenth Amendment, which secured the voting rights of all men regardless of race, color, or previous enslavement.

Soon, there were impressive strides made by the freedmen. Making up a large percentage of the population in the South, blacks soon won state elections and seats in the US Congress. Laws were passed against discrimination on public transportation and for programs to boost the economic situation of black people. "For the first time, African Americans voted in large numbers and held public office at every level of government. It was a remarkable, unprecedented effort to build an interracial democracy on the ashes of slavery," says Eric Foner, a Columbia University professor of history.[2]

Reconstruction

Reconstruction saw both ups and downs for former slaves. Many found their families, which had often been torn apart by slave auctions and individual sales of slaves to other plantation owners. Together, they began to build lives as freedmen and women. Blacks established their own churches, which would become an important community support for decades to come. However, few had the opportunity to buy land. Instead, many worked for their former owners, often as sharecroppers. As sharecroppers, men and women could rent their own piece of a landowner's property and earn a portion, or share, of the money for crops produced on it; however, conditions improved only slightly between freed people and their former owners.

To make matters worse, many white Southerners refused to accept the changes the end of the war and Reconstruction brought. The KKK and other white supremacist groups materialized during this time. To keep the South the way they wanted it, they used violence and intimidated local Republican leaders and any African Americans who refused to accept their authority. Civil War General Ulysses S. Grant, elected president in 1868, after Andrew Johnson, attempted to squash the violence by sending troops to these areas and passing legislation. Unfortunately, it wasn't enough to keep these groups from slowly reclaiming many government positions in 1874 and 1876, sometimes through violence.

In 1877, Republican Rutherford B. Hayes ran for president and won—but only because he had cut a deal with the Democrats of the South to allow them to control it. With his election, Reconstruction was over.

Biding Their Time in the South

Living in the South became a downward spiral for African Americans seeking equality with their white neighbors. Some black leaders in the late 1800s and early 1900s, such as Booker T. Washington, encouraged blacks to "bide their time" and focus on gaining an education and financial independence, and thereby become respected by whites. Over the next two decades, this became increasingly difficult, however, as more limitations were thrust upon them.

A family of sharecroppers poses for a photo in 1910. Sharecropping, which gave workers more autonomy than working for white people, was the main way black families in the South earned a living after the Civil War.

"Jim Crow" was a derogatory term for a black man. Many Southern laws, called Jim Crow laws, were passed that enforced segregation between blacks and whites. Many of these "laws" said that the two races should be kept separate as long as the facilities for both were equal. The facilities in question included schools, churches, restaurants, and public bathrooms. Within eating establishments, public transportation, theaters, and other public places, blacks were required to sit in separate areas or even outside.

Black facilities, however, were rarely equal to what the whites used. This was evident in many places, especially in black Southern schools. Many were pieced together by determined educators with the help of the community, and they scraped by with little money and supplies for their students.

Sharecropping became a way for people to earn a living in the South. Many preferred this to working directly for the landowner because they had more freedom and did not have to endure the harsh supervision that they had experienced as slaves. Sharecropping was not always beneficial, though. Sometimes crops failed. Other times, they prospered. Because of this uncertainty, some black families were able to save enough money to buy their own land, while others grew more in debt to their landowners. This was especially true as the price of cotton, the South's main crop, fell lower over the years.

Keeping Power

To maintain power over blacks, whites would accuse them of false crimes, especially the rape of white women. This often resulted in lynching—the public, ruthless hanging and killing of individuals, all without a trial. It was often committed by a mob of white people, and black individuals were the victims.

Black people who defended themselves against false accusations or refused to accept discrimination might also become targets of a lynch mob.

It was in this rural Southern climate of disadvantage that 90 percent of black people lived after the war. Limited job options meant that many of them spent their days doing backbreaking work. That left very little personal time for grooming or recreation. How former slaves had maintained their hair during slavery continued during the post-war era. Most women kept their hair braided and covered until Sundays. Men frequently shaved their heads or kept their hair close-cut for convenience. This would change, however, as more people adapted new habits and more entrepreneurs focused on advantages for the African American community.

Fighting White Power

From the start of the Jim Crow era, there were those who chose not to "bide their time" but instead worked to improve their lives. Some fought within the system to change the laws through court challenges, journalism, and civil rights activism.

Often referred to as fearless, Ida B. Wells-Barnett was one who fought within the system. Born during the Civil War as a slave, she and her siblings were later educated in a school created by the Freedmen's Bureau. She became a teacher herself and secured a job teaching near Memphis, Tennessee.

On a train ride back to Memphis in 1884, she bought a first-class ticket. This area was in the front section of the train—the white section. She was ordered to go to the colored car but refused. She was forcefully removed, but she sued the railcar company. A former Union soldier served as the judge, and he ruled in her favor, saying that the colored car was not

Activist and journalist Ida B. Wells-Barnett challenged the separate but equal mandate and then investigated the practice of lynching. Her work and activism was instrumental in the anti-lynching movement.

the first-class accommodations she had paid for. However, the ruling was overturned in an appeals court, greatly disheartening Wells-Barnett and others seeking equal treatment.

This was not the last of Mrs. Wells-Barnett, however, as she wrote about discrimination in a black newspaper while she taught. Eventually, she was fired from her school because of what she wrote in the paper. This spurred her into a career as a journalist. She went on to investigate and write about lynching, finding that most people lynched were innocent of the crimes they were accused of. Her work helped propel the anti-lynching movement that started in the 1890s. "The way to right wrongs," she wrote, "is to turn the light of truth upon them."[3]

Plessy v. Ferguson

As segregation spread, even New Orleans, Louisiana—known for being racially integrated—fell into step with the "separate but equal" mandate permeating the 1890s. The city instituted separate railcars for blacks and whites on its railroads. However, some people thought this went against the Fourteenth Amendment, which guarantees rights to all, regardless of race. The New Orleans black community decided to test the legality of the amendment. Homer Plessy, a man of mixed race, agreed to attempt to board a white railcar in June 1892. When told to move to the black car, he refused and was arrested. He was found guilty of violating the local law, and the US Supreme Court eventually heard the case. The case's name has been synonymous with "separate but equal" since: *Plessy v. Ferguson.*

In 1896, the Supreme Court ruled that the "separate but equal" rule instituted by many towns in the South was constitutional on interstate railroads and that the Fourteenth Amendment only applied to political and civil rights, not "social rights." The judges stated that separate but equal did not imply that black people were inferior but treated the same, in their own spheres. This set a precedent for many areas of life for decades to come.

New Places of Refuge

While some were trying to make change from within the white system, others chose to embrace segregation completely. Instead of being on the sidelines of white communities, they chose to create their own.

African Americans had already shown that they could establish strongholds for themselves, most often in the churches and schools that they built up over the years. Many skilled blacks found themselves sought-after tradesmen for both white and black customers. Some blacks started successful businesses, but bad things sometimes happened to them if competing white business owners believed they were becoming too prosperous.

Some people believed the way around this was to create towns that were just for black people—not simply being segregated to different parts of existing facilities or areas of a town.

From 1877 to 1879, Benjamin "Pap" Singleton led three hundred black people to Kansas to start their own community. Kansas was chosen because it was where abolitionist John Brown had attempted to fight slavery in the 1850s. It was also a nonslave state before the Civil War. Singleton believed it would be his people's new promised land, and that is how he described it to those seeking brighter days.

Others followed his example as twenty thousand African Americans moved to Kansas the following year. Unfortunately, many people in this second wave were not financially ready for the move and came in large groups, which resulted in these new communities seeking assistance from the state.

Some who headed to Kansas stopped in Saint Louis, Missouri, along the way and chose to stay there instead of continuing to the Sunflower State. The city developed a robust black community and cultural scene, which would have attracted those seeking better opportunities for work other than agriculture.

Others who wanted all-black communities didn't want to leave the South to make them a reality. One such town to arise was Davis Bend, Mississippi. Founded by Benjamin Montgomery in 1865, it was a large cooperative community bought from a plantation owner. After Benjamin died in 1879, his son Isaiah continued to lead Davis Bend. Before long, though, it started to decline due to a combination of poor farming conditions, falling crop prices, and bad political conditions. When seventy residents left for Kansas, Isaiah Montgomery decided to build a black town himself. In 1887, he and eleven other people founded Mound Bayou.

Later called "the Jewel of the Delta" by President Theodore Roosevelt, Mound Bayou, Mississippi, began as 840 acres (340 hectares) of swampland with dense forests. Building on a foundation of pride in being black, education, and economic opportunities, the community worked to attract highly skilled people. "They wanted the most highly educated people who were entrepreneurial, who were going to come in and contribute something to making this community even more competitive, even better," said Dr. Rolando Herts, director of the Delta Center for Culture and Learning.[4]

Churches, stores, and schools sprang up as the town's prosperity grew from its agriculture- and railroad-based

Benjamin Montgomery, a mechanic and inventor, founded the all-black town of Davis Bend, Mississippi. After his death, his son Isaiah built another town that was dubbed the "Jewel of the Delta," Mound Bayou, Mississippi.

economy. Famous black educator Booker T. Washington praised the town's accomplishments and shared Montgomery's segregationist ideas. However, not all was blissful. The safety of Mound Bayou's residents from white supremacists, for instance, came at a cost. Montgomery used his political clout to suppress black voting in Mississippi in exchange for the safety of the town. This meant residents could not and did not vote in elections, denying them a right guaranteed by the Fifteenth Amendment.

The population and prosperity of Mound Bayou declined after 1915 due to the large number of blacks leaving the

South and the falling price of cotton. The town still exists today, though it is a shadow of what it once was.

Striving for Equality

As the twentieth century dawned and the country's progressive era of rapid growth and migration was going strong, many African Americans chose a different path to safety and opportunity: groups aimed at financial development, civil rights, and fair treatment. These included the National Association of Colored Women, the National Negro Business League, and more. Soon, these had members numbering in the thousands.

One such organization was the National Association for the Advancement of Colored People (NAACP). Founded in 1909, it was unusual in that progressive white activists started it. The group quickly made black educator and author W. E. B. Du Bois the director of publication and research. The NAACP rallied against lynching as well as making change through lawsuits and political pressure. In the 1950s, they would help bring *Brown v. Board of Education of Topeka* to court as they challenged school segregation. The case went before the US Supreme Court in 1954, with the NAACP's Thurgood Marshall as chief attorney.

Marshall told the court that the South's system of segregation represented "an inherent determination that the people who were formerly in slavery, regardless of anything else, shall be kept as near that stage as is possible. Now is the time, we submit, that the court should make it clear that this is not what our Constitution stands for."[5]

The court agreed and ruled in favor of desegregating schools. This decision fueled the civil rights movement of the 1950s and 1960s.

A HAIRY BUSINESS

Embracing natural black hairstyles has become more common in Western culture, and today many African Americans take pride in well-groomed hair. Due to slavery, however, this was not always the case in the United States.

Most slaves came from West Africa, where elaborate hairstyles were common and often told details about the wearer, such as marital status, religion, wealth, age, and more. Some hairstyles were even developed to show that a man was preparing for war or that a young woman was too young to marry. Despite how the hair was styled, the health of the hair was important too. "A woman with long, thick hair demonstrates the life-force, the multiplying power of profusion, prosperity, a 'green thumb' for raising bountiful farms and many healthy children," explains anthropologist Sylvia Ardyn Boone, speaking of West African communities.[6]

When slave traders kidnapped Africans to sell as slaves, they shaved their heads. There were some sanitary reasons for this, but it also was a way to take away part of the person's identity.

In America, slaves often did not have time to maintain the beauty and hygiene routines of their homeland, unless they did jobs near or around the slave owner and his or her family and needed to look more presentable. Infections from ringworm and lice were common. Lack of proper hygiene, along with stress and poor diet, caused scalp disease and hair loss.

Things improved somewhat after 1808, when it became illegal to import slaves from Africa. The slaves in America couldn't be replaced with new ones from Africa, so some owners decided to care for them better. Many were given Sundays off for church, rest, and self-care. Yet for many, hair problems continued even after slavery was abolished. This was due to lack of knowledge, resources, or time.

As stronger black communities developed after Reconstruction, many black women sought to have hair that was more socially acceptable. Some

These men and women working in a field illustrate examples of how many African Americans wore their hair in the nineteenth century.

black families had extra money to spend on grooming and hygiene. This opened the way for black hair-care entrepreneurs such as Madam C.J. Walker to shine. Through Walker's efforts—as well as those of some of her primary competitors—many black women started to take pride in their appearance again.

CHAPTER TWO

Becoming Madam Walker

Madam C.J. Walker is often billed as the first black, female, self-made millionaire in America. In actuality, her finances did not quite total a million dollars. Nevertheless, she created the Madam C.J. Walker Manufacturing Company, a hair-care empire that helped black women care for their hair. She also found ways to use her influence to help other women become financially independent and take pride in their appearances. What's even more amazing is that she did this in just twelve years.

The business of beauty made Madam C.J. Walker rich beyond her dreams, but it did not blind her from

Driving her automobiles, such as this Pope-Waverly Coupe, was a pleasure afforded Madam C.J. Walker by her wealth.

her roots or the lack of opportunity for black women in the United States. She would often say to her sales agents, "To be beautiful does not refer alone to the arrangement of the hair, the perfection of the complexion or to the beauty of the form. To be beautiful, one must combine these qualities with a beautiful mind and soul."[1]

The First Born Free

Before she became Madam C.J. Walker, she was simply Sarah Breedlove. Breedlove was born on December 23, 1867. She was the first child born free to parents Owen and Minerva Breedlove. Siblings Louvenia, Owen Jr., Alexander, and James had all been born as slaves. The family lived in a cabin on a rented plot of land in Delta, Louisiana. They had lived there as slaves and still worked the land and picked cotton in 1867, as they had before they were free. Whether their youngest daughter being born free gave them some hope for the future is hard to know, but her father was eligible to vote for the first time just months before she was born. Reconstruction efforts were going strong, and many blacks were elected to office.

This promising period did not last long. Breedlove was still an infant when violence aimed at both black and white Republicans began—violence from white Democrats trying to take back power in the South. This violence included assault, arson, and even murder. Despite this, the Breedloves saw some prosperity, as cotton crops did well that year and the next. In 1869, her parents welcomed a baby boy, Solomon, and were able to pay the $100 required to legally marry.

Breedlove's childhood combined working alongside her parents in the fields, playing with friends and catching crawfish, and attending church. Most black schools in the area had been shut down due to violence aimed at them, so she had almost no formal education. Minerva died in 1873, and Owen remarried. However, not long after, he died too. Little is known about Owen's second wife, but Breedlove did not live with her after her father's death. Seven-year-old Breedlove instead went to live with her sister and her brother-in-law, who made her go to work doing laundry by hand for those who could pay for the service.

During this time, blacks were being subjected to Jim Crow laws, designed to take away many of their freedoms and opportunities. Some African Americans left the South and headed toward the promise of all-black towns starting in Kansas. Breedlove's older brother Alexander was one of them, but he did not reach Kansas. Instead, he stayed in Saint Louis, Missouri, and became a barber. Brothers Owen Jr. and James soon followed him.

Breedlove married Moses McWilliams when she was just fourteen. Later, she admitted she did it to have a home of her own. Her biographers have suggested that she also wanted to get away from her brother-in-law, Jesse Powell, who often mistreated her.

In June 1885, she gave birth to her only child, a daughter named Lelia. "So long deprived of her own mother's touch," wrote her great-great-granddaughter A'Lelia Bundles, "Sarah had had little exposure to the overwhelming, all-consuming maternal protectiveness that Lelia stirred in her. For the rest of her life, Lelia remained the center of her affection, the source of her motivation."[2]

Her new family life was short lived when McWilliams died in 1888. Breedlove did not return to her sister and brother-in-law's home for help. Instead, she planned to leave Mississippi and follow her brothers' footsteps to Missouri.

Saint Louis and Up

Once she and Lelia arrived in Saint Louis, Breedlove quickly went to work as a laundress, earning $4 to $12 a week. She found support and help in the St. Paul African Methodist Episcopal Church. This church was a stronghold of educated black leaders working to help others. She was offered an education for Lelia at a nearby school for orphans, and she accepted. Already, the city was offering more opportunity than her home state ever had.

Over the next ten years, she continued working hard as a laundress. She married John Davis in 1894, but their marriage was filled with problems. They moved often, and Breedlove hoped to find a way out of her life of backbreaking labor. One morning, while doing laundry, she paused and considered who would take care of her and her daughter when she was too old to work like this. "This set me to thinking," she said later, "but with all my thinking I couldn't see how I, a poor washerwoman, was going to better my condition."[3]

In spite of all her struggles, Breedlove kept Lelia in school, and her daughter graduated in 1901. Wanting to keep Lelia away from the bars and clubs that were becoming prominent, or from leading a life such as her own, Breedlove took on even more work. Eventually, she saved enough money to send her daughter to Knoxville College in Tennessee, which provided high school- and college-level education.

In the two years that followed, two of her brothers died, and her last living brother, Owen, abandoned his family. This left her support system in a mess, which became worse when she and Davis ended their marriage in 1903 (although they were never legally divorced). During this stressful period, Breedlove began experiencing hair loss. She handled the

In 1889, Walker moved to Saint Louis to be closer to her brothers. It has changed greatly since she lived there but continues to be a city of opportunity.

problem the same way black women had in the South for decades: she covered it with a head wrap.

She soon began to see Charles Joseph Walker, or C.J., who worked in advertising and news. He was said to be charming, well dressed, and ambitious. Being with him may have encouraged her to find a solution to her hair problem. She said she had tried anything that was suggested to her as a possible cure, but they all had failed.

Later, she would tell how she discovered her famous hair-growing formula in a fanciful story. In it, she prayed for guidance and was delivered an answer through a dream: a black man appeared and told her what ingredients from

Africa to mix together to save her hair. She said she ordered the ingredients, followed the divine instructions, and was rewarded with a hair-saving ointment. Then, she decided to sell it and help other black women struggling as she had.

A more likely story is the one related by Annie Turnbo Malone, who had moved to Saint Louis in 1902 to start a hairdressing business. Her specialty was treating scalps and growing hair. Unlike other products at the time, Malone's would have healed and conditioned hair and scalps instead of drying them. She also taught women to shampoo more often. Malone claimed that she had treated Breedlove's hair. Neither woman's claims can be proven, but what is known is that Breedlove was one of Malone's earliest sales agents for her company, Poro. Breedlove started with the company in 1903.

On the Road to Success

Becoming a Poro agent gave Breedlove a taste of success she had seen little of in her life. In 1905, she moved to Denver, Colorado, where her sister-in-law lived. In hand, she had a case of Malone's hair treatment. There, she set up shop as a Poro sales agent. She also worked as a cook but sold hair treatment on the side. In November, Walker joined her, and they were married in January. In spring of 1906, Breedlove began placing newspaper ads as Malone's sales agent with her new married name, Mrs. C.J. Walker. Her husband began working in real estate and entertainment. They supported each other's business goals, and they flourished.

Walker began to experiment with mixing her own treatment. Soon, she stopped selling Malone's products and introduced her own, as Madam C.J. Walker's Wonderful

Hair Grower. Adding "Madam" to her husband's name was a common tactic for hairdressers at the time, and the name Madam C.J. Walker was one that would last well into history. Before long, business boomed, and Walker also offered scalp treatment classes. Lelia eventually moved to Denver to join her mother's business.

Malone attempted to call out Walker, claiming that she had stolen her formula. Walker's Denver clients came to her defense, however. Malone eventually sent another agent to Denver as Walker and her husband were traveling to grow Walker's competing business. The couple focused their travels on the South, where Walker believed the new company would find a good market. She was right. In 1907, she earned $3,652—more than ten times what she earned as a laundress.

The Walkers also had a mail-order side to the business. This allowed people to order their products through the mail rather than at a store. The Walkers realized they needed a place to operate the business from. After visiting New York and Pennsylvania, they chose Pittsburgh, Pennsylvania, because of its many railroads that could supply convenient shipping all over the United States.

Walker's clever marketing using her own story, along with her hard work and ambition, drove her business even further forward. She used photographs of her now-beautiful tresses and how she got them. Black women, eager for a way to move up in society, saw fixing their hair as part of the solution. They were attracted to Walker and her manner, which focused on making her clientele feel better about themselves. In 1908, her income almost doubled from the previous year.

She trained dozens of sales agents in Pittsburgh, and Lelia kept them supplied with products. Eventually, she sent Lelia on the road in the hopes that she would eventually know enough

Walker's line of products was started in 1906. Some products, including the Scalp Ointment and Glossine advertised here, sold for decades after the entrepreneur's death. Providing a positive body image for black women was key to her marketing success.

to take over the business. Lelia took this on, but a year later, in 1909, she married John Robinson. A job on the road was difficult for a newly married couple. Soon after their marriage, it was decided the newlyweds would stay in Pittsburgh, where Lelia would run a supply station for the company's agents, and Madam Walker would go back on the road.

In 1910, Walker had great ambitions for her company: She wanted a place to build a permanent headquarters, offer stock options for her company, and to create a factory. She reached out to educator and leader Booker T. Washington, but he dismissed her idea, saying he had no time to assist her. While visiting with her sister-in-law, Walker began to realize her husband might have been misusing company funds. Despite this, she stayed with him.

Upon visiting Indianapolis, Indiana, the Walkers chose the city as the site of their new headquarters. The city was called the Crossroads of America, and it had a variety of industry, making it ideal for a growing company. Walker bought a two-story brick home and enlisted the help of two legal advisors. By the end of the year, she had made more than $10,000, the equivalent of $250,000 in 2018.

Though the company was growing by leaps and bounds, the Walker women were not faring as well in their personal lives. Walker and her husband were becoming less connected, and Robinson left Lelia after a year of marriage.

In 1911, Walker made the Madam C.J. Walker Manufacturing Company of Indiana an incorporated business. This meant that the company became its own legal entity apart from the Walkers.

Generosity and Perseverance

Despite gaining wealth, Madam Walker did not hoard her money. She was known as a giving person who helped the poorest among her neighbors. Whether it was aiding people with rent or groceries or giving change to children, she was driven to help those who were so much like she had been not too many years before. Her factory alone kept three dozen people well employed. Despite this, she longed to make a broader and more lasting impact on the black community.

Though Indianapolis was much more wholesome of a city than Saint Louis, it still had its bars and gambling halls that could lure the underemployed into a worse situation than they were already in. In 1911, Walker began supporting the Young Men's Christian Association, or YMCA, in its effort to build a facility to provide a better place for black men to go. She was the first person to pledge $1,000 (over $26,600 in 2018) to the fundraiser. She continued to support the organization and its female counterpart, the YWCA, for the rest of her life.

In the coming years, she continued to push a connection with Booker T. Washington and the school he ran, the Tuskegee Institute. Washington was reluctant to encourage a business relationship with her because he did not believe hairdressing was a key career to uplift black people. Plus, he and many other African Americans disliked that she and her competitors sold hair-straightening products and systems. They believed black people should not try to fit the beauty norms of white people. Based on this, he disagreed with allowing hairdressers and cosmetic manufacturers into his National Negro Business League, which worked to enhance the business and financial development of black people.

Walker was nothing if not persistent, however. "Perseverance is my motto," she said. "It laid the Atlantic cable, it gave us the telegraph, telephone, and wireless. It gave to the world an Abraham Lincoln, and to a race freedom."[4] With a strong backbone, she came uninvited to Tuskegee—and Washington's private home there—during the 1912 Negro Farmers' Conference. Again, Washington denied her the chance to speak at the conference, but he did allow her to speak to a smaller audience at the school's chapel. Undaunted, she took the opportunity in stride.

Personal matters, however, were distracting Walker. Her marriage to her husband had long been suffering from C.J.'s mismanagement of business funds as well as affairs he had with other women. Also in 1912, Walker decided to file for divorce.

Though disappointed by two different men, she would soon find more supportive ground at the National Association of Colored Women's Convention held that summer. Opening the convention was educator Mary McLeod Bethune, who was the head of the Daytona Normal and Industrial Institute, which provided black girls a traditional, vocational, and home economics education. Walker volunteered to lead a fundraiser for the school, possibly noting the similarities between Bethune and herself. She was also formally introduced to the group, who had just named Margaret Murray Washington, Booker T. Washington's wife, the group's president. Surely, now Washington would not ignore her.

However, he continued to snub her at the annual meeting of the National Negro Business League. After publisher George Knox, who was a friend to both Walker and Washington, introduced her, Washington rudely dismissed the introduction. Walker's patience ran out. She stood from her seat and addressed Washington directly. "Surely, you are not going to shut the door in my face," she said, and then summarized her rise from cotton fields to businesswoman of an industry that did not always get respect. "Now, my object in life is not simply to make money for myself or to spend it on myself in dressing or running around in an automobile. But I love to use a part of what I make in trying to help others."[5] She finished by declaring her goal was to open an industrial school in Africa. Though Knox's newspaper, the *Freeman*, declared her speech a highlight of the convention, it would take time for Washington to warm up to her.

The Walker Manufacturing Company continued to grow, with about one thousand sales agents as well as the employees

Walker, with publisher George Knox (*first on left*), Booker T. Washington (*center left*), and other community leaders, poses at the dedication of the Indianapolis YMCA in 1913.

at her headquarters. As her company expanded, so too did her real-estate investments and her philanthropic gestures.

Construction on the YMCA building was finished in 1913, and a celebratory event was held to honor the occasion. Walker invited Booker T. Washington to be her houseguest during his stay for the event. He accepted, and during his address at the dedication, he singled her out as one of the largest donors for the project. This was the beginning of Walker's support of Tuskegee, and Washington began to include her in some events. When she asked him to consider adding her hairdressing course to Tuskegee's curriculum, however, he declined but did so more kindly than in the past. But just as their relationship was starting to warm up, Washington died in 1915.

A Growing Business and Worrisome Health

"Having a good article for the market is one thing," Walker once told the *New York Age*, "and putting it properly before the public is another."[6] Though a great marketer and self-promoter, Walker put in many hours and miles to ensure her company's success. Between 1913 and 1919, she traveled in her touring car almost constantly, to speaking engagements as well as to train sales agents. She expanded the business internationally, too—to Jamaica, Haiti, Costa Rica, Cuba and Panama—traveling to most of these countries as well. As she had become more active in helping charities and activist groups like the NAACP and the anti-lynching movement, she encouraged her sales agents to do the same.

Meanwhile, she was becoming frustrated with the racial limitations in Indianapolis. In 1914, an incident at the Isis Theatre in town sparked her anger. The theater began charging black moviegoers twenty-five cents while maintaining a fifteen-cent price for white customers. Though she asked her lawyer to sue, it is unclear if the case ever went to court. Walker kept her business headquarters in the city, but soon she began looking for a place to put a permanent home, in New York.

In late 1916, in the midst of her hectic travel schedule, Walker became ill. The doctor was so concerned about her high blood pressure, he insisted she clear her schedule and take a six-week rest. Heeding his advice, she decided to go to

Hot Springs, Arkansas, a place known for its healing thermal springs. However, the rest brought relief, not a cure. It turned out Walker was overexerted due to her busy schedule. That, combined with hypertension and an undiagnosed kidney disease, was the root of the problem. Once she left Hot Springs, her busy lifestyle continued, and so did her health problems.

Still looking for a permanent home, Walker bought land in an upscale area known as Irvington-on-Hudson in New York. Twenty miles (32 kilometers) north of the city of Manhattan, some of the wealthiest people lived there. In fact, the property was close to the estate of oil tycoon John D. Rockefeller. There, Walker began working with the first registered black architect in New York, Vertner Woodson Tandy. Not only did she want the perfect house but also a place that would function as a conference center. After two years of construction, the result was the lavish estate she called Villa Lewaro.

That fall, Walker's health was getting progressively worse. Her kidney disease was diagnosed, and the doctor recommended she enter rehabilitation at the Battle Creek Sanitarium in Michigan. There, the entrepreneur was prescribed a bland vegetarian diet, exercise, and water therapy. On top of that, the doctors said she should never work again. "This is necessary for all time and means she must give little or no attention again to business or heavy social activities," her assistant wrote to the company's lawyer.[7]

Of course, Walker could only handle a few weeks of bean soup and vegetables before she was right back in New York to oversee her company and the construction of her mansion. She and Lelia enjoyed their Christmas season together—a happy time before an intense year to come.

Walker sales agents pose in front of Villa Lewaro at a national convention in 1924. Building an organized sales force that also promoted social welfare was a goal Madam C.J. Walker achieved in 1917, just two years before her death.

The Final Years

In April 1917, the United States declared war on Germany and entered World War I, which had been happening in Europe since 1914. Many in the nation were caught up in a wave of patriotism, including many African Americans. Walker joined the board of the Circle for Negro War Relief, an organization created so black women could aid black soldiers (at first, they weren't allowed to volunteer for the American Red Cross). Lelia also volunteered for several wartime committees and organized fundraisers.

FAMILY AND BUSINESS: A VOLATILE MIX

Mother-daughter relationships are often complicated, and the rags-to-riches life of Madam Walker and her daughter Lelia made their relationship even more tumultuous.

Lelia, who would later go by A'Lelia, started life as modestly as her mother had, but with one difference: an education. During Lelia's late childhood, Walker had been married to John Davis, a poor father figure who added to the family's troubles. Though Walker ensured that Lelia's education continued into college, she quickly brought her adult daughter on board when the hair-product company took off.

After her divorce from C.J. Walker was finalized in 1912, Walker and Lelia realized that they had no heir for the company. Lelia, age twenty-seven, had been separated from her husband for two years with no reconciliation in sight. Their solution was for Lelia to adopt a thirteen-year-old girl named Faery Mae Bryant. Bryant had spent summers and holidays visiting her grandmother, who knew Walker and lived near her company in Indianapolis. Bryant wasn't actually an orphan, but her widowed mother knew the adoption would provide opportunities for Faery Mae that she couldn't provide. After the adoption, she went by the name Mae Walker and often traveled with Walker as a hair model.

Though Lelia would never have the drive and instinct of her mother, she wished to be independent. She supervised operations in Pittsburgh and then the New York City area, eventually gaining some international territory. Despite this, the two constantly bickered over money and business decisions.

Company attorney F.B. Ransom frequently acted as the buffer between the two passionate women. At one point, Lelia called her mother an "impulsive baby." Later, considering how often her mother was gone on business, her tone would become mournful, "With all this big house and a nice income and above all a wonderful mother, I am so alone in the world."[8]

Their life was not all troubles, and they enjoyed the social life that their wealth provided them. The two also loved shopping, and Madam Walker had difficulty refusing her daughter anything. Some theorize this was due to Walker's guilt over being gone so much and Lelia's rough childhood. After her

Lelia Walker, shown here circa 1927, had a relationship with her mother that was both contentious and adoring. However, she struggled to achieve independence working for her mother.

mother died, Lelia changed her name to A'Lelia and became a hostess of many of the artists of the Harlem Renaissance.

In the end, mother and daughter both lived much of their lives for the Walker Manufacturing Company. They were each married three times but neither experienced a successful marriage. They both also directed their daughters' lives to some degree. While Madam C.J. Walker always encouraged Lelia and pushed her at times, Lelia pushed Mae into marrying Dr. Gordon Jackson, the grandson of a wealthy black coal dealer—though Mae divorced him after three years and later eloped with Marion Perry. Both had larger-than-life personalities and achievements that far outshone their roots.

Early the next year, Walker was back to a busy schedule with a three-month tour to grow the business, plus visiting military camps and promoting the Circle for Negro War Relief. As her health continued to decline, she was more determined to keep up her packed schedule. She delved into politics as well, trying to influence the Paris peace talks as the war ended later that year, and discussing the status of African colonies that were ruled by Germany. She attempted to obtain a passport to attend the peace talks, but the Military Intelligence Division had identified her and others, such as journalist Ida B. Wells-Barnett, as possible agitators. Their passports were denied.

Disappointed by the government's intrusion in their efforts, Walker refocused on her company and her daughter, including taking over the New York operations of the company so Lelia could travel and develop trade with the Caribbean and Central and South America. The anti-lynching campaign and the NAACP also occupied her mind and efforts. "My desire now is to do more than ever for my race. I would love to live for them. I've caught the vision. I can see what they need," she said.[9] By Eastertime 1919, however, Walker's health was in decline despite her drive.

She returned home after Easter with little hope of getting better. She updated her will, ensuring her daughter would receive all her real-estate holdings and one-third of the company's profits. The remaining two-thirds profit would maintain Villa Lewaro and be given to "worthy" charities. She left large sums for family members and close friends, as well as charities and schools, including the Tuskegee Institute, Mary McLeod Bethune's school, and the YMCAs and YWCAs in Saint Louis and New York City.

Walker was temporarily buoyed by the news from overseas that Lelia, then traveling in Panama, had accepted a marriage proposal from suitor James Kennedy. She was strong enough to dictate a letter congratulating her daughter and asking her to come home. Before Lelia could return from Panama via boat, Walker slipped into unconsciousness. On the morning of May 25, 1919, she drew her last breath.

The funeral was scheduled for May 30, so Lelia might make it, but sadly, her train wouldn't arrive until the day after.

One of Walker's dreams had been to achieve the status of a millionaire. Though many newspapers at the time called her one, the value of her estate when she died was closer to $600,000. Today's equivalent would be almost $9 million. However, she was the sole owner of her company, which was worth more than one million dollars alone. The worth of the employment she provided for forty thousand women, the self-esteem of black women, and her charitable and business example were worth far more. "She had an indomitable spirit that prevailed through the difficulties of finding capital, and through the difficulties of her own very limited social position," said Harvard Business School historian Nancy F. Koehn. "In a market in which there weren't many realms where women could play, she found a way."[10]

COPYRIGH
A.P. BEDO
N.O. La.

CHAPTER THREE

Competitors and Colleagues

Madam Walker's success and legacy is due in part to the era in which she lived, when black people were striving to overcome Jim Crow laws and attain the freedom they had won. Though a self-made millionaire, Walker worked with other black leaders of the time to give her company an edge while trying to better the black community. Some people supported her while others were not so enthused by her actions.

Annie Turnbo Malone

Annie Turnbo Malone had an unlikely start for a future entrepreneur. Her father fought for the Union in the

Educator Booker T. Washington often rode on horseback on the Tuskegee Institute's campus to see how things were doing.

Civil War while her mother fled from Kentucky to Illinois with their two children. Malone was born later, in 1869. Her parents died when she was young, so her older sister raised her.

Though described as a sickly child, Malone attended high school, where she discovered a love of chemistry. She also had an affinity for grooming and styling her sisters' hair. These two interests combined to bring her success in the black hair-care industry.

In 1900, Malone and her sister moved to Lovejoy, Illinois, one of the all-black communities founded after the Civil War. There, the Turnbo sisters offered hair treatments to women, and Malone became known for helping to heal and rejuvenate the scalps and hair of black women.

In 1902, Malone moved to a bigger market for her services and products: Saint Louis, Missouri. The city was growing and preparing for the 1904 World's Fair, a large international exhibit. It also had a strong black population and community. She made her treatments and sold them door-to-door. Eventually, she named her company Poro Products.

To expand her market, Malone spent nine months touring the South. There, she began to gather others to help promote her company. She used a popular pyramid strategy of training sales agents that would then sell her products and find more agents. The Poro agents could earn more money by recruiting more women to be trained as agents. Those who successfully completed a Poro training course could open an official Poro salon. Malone grew her business in the United States as well as in the Caribbean and in Latin America.

In 1903, she met and trained washerwoman Sarah Breedlove to be one of her sales agents. As orphans who had lived with their siblings, the two had some common ground.

Annie Turnbo Malone not only helped pave the way for black hair care manufacturers but also trained Walker as one of her sales agents before Walker started her own company.

However, a couple years later, Breedlove remarried and started her own business as Madam C.J. Walker. The two women became competitors, with Malone suggesting that Walker had stolen her Wonderful Hair Grower formula.

Like Walker, Malone used her success to help other black women become independent and feel more confident by helping improve their self-image. She used incentives to encourage women to complete her training program. One of her proud achievements was creating Poro College in 1917.

The college was much more than a college, however. It was for training hairstylists and sales agents as well as a space for the arts, lectures, a chapel, and a gym. "Poro College is consecrated to the uplift of humanity—race women in particular," Malone said.[1] Beyond her business, Malone founded an orphanage and made large contributions to the Saint Louis Colored YMCA.

Poro Products peaked in 1918 when the company had 240 employees and more than sixty-eight thousand sales agents across the country. When the Great Depression started in 1929, the Poro Company was hit hard, as everyday people struggled to pay for basic necessities. Afterward, white-owned companies took advantage of the struggling Poro Products and its competitors' weakened state to take over the black hair-care industry.

Aaron Malone, Malone's third husband, is another key reason behind the erosion of her company. They married in 1914 and were partners in the business, but their marriage took a downturn as early as 1921. As he had been named president, her husband tried to take control of the company. Six years later, Malone divorced him and was able to keep her company after a long divorce, but the company and her reputation were damaged.

The company continued but was seized in 1951 for failure to pay taxes. Malone died in 1957 with little continuing legacy. Unlike Walker, Malone's personality was more reserved, and the public didn't connect with her on a personal level like they did with Walker. Also, Malone's divorce from her third husband tarnished her reputation as well as hurt her business. In the end, her business model and the orphanage she helped to build stood as testaments to her work and desire to help the black community.

Mary McLeod Bethune

Like so many of the black leaders during Walker's time, educator and social activist Mary McLeod Bethune was a free child born to former slaves. She did not let that define her, however. Born July 10, 1875, Bethune and her family—she had sixteen siblings, most of them older—worked in her family's cotton fields and could pick 250 pounds (113 kilograms) of cotton a day.

When a school started nearby, her family could only afford to send one child, and they picked her. An educator at heart, she would come home and teach her siblings and parents what she had learned. She earned a scholarship to attend Scotia Seminary for Girls in North Carolina, where she discovered her talents for singing and public speaking.

After graduating, she wanted to be a missionary in Africa. She received another scholarship to attend the Moody Bible Institute in Chicago. Though the only black student there, she did not encounter racism until after graduation, when the Presbyterian Church's mission program wouldn't accept her because of her color. Disappointed, she turned to education, teaching at several mission schools in the South. In 1898, she married another teacher, Albertus Bethune. Their marriage lasted eight years, and they had one son.

In 1904, she returned to education by renting a four-room house in Florida to start a school for girls. The school, the Daytona Normal and Industrial Institute, grew from five to 250 students in two years. Early on, Bethune focused on practical, vocational training, falling in line with the kind of curriculum that Booker T. Washington promoted. Bethune believed that her students needed to learn how to be better wives and mothers, in addition to reading and math, in order

A friend of Madam Walker's, Mary McLeod Bethune was a powerful educator and activist. She also served as the director of the Division of Negro Affairs under President Franklin Roosevelt.

to improve future generations. She also sought donations from prosperous white families such as the Rockefellers, Gambles, and Roosevelts. These two things earned her some criticism from black intellectuals of the time, but she held firm in doing whatever it took to provide education for her community. "My people needed literacy ... but they needed even more to learn the simples of farming, of making decent homes, of health and plain cleanliness," Bethune said.[2]

In the beginning, the school was supported by the community through modest means such as chicken dinners. As time went on, Bethune found more financial backers for her cause. Later, the school merged with the Cookman Institute for Men to create the Bethune-Cookman College, with Bethune as the president. Bethune served as the college's president until 1942, but that was just a part of her accomplishments and the reach of her work.

There were no hospitals in Daytona, Florida, that would admit a black person. So, she started a hospital on Bethune-Cookman's grounds. It quickly grew from a two-bed to twenty-six-bed facility and was in operation for twenty years, until the city hospital opened a wing for black people.

Bethune joined the National Association of Colored Women and at one time served as its president. In 1912, Bethune made her first appearance at the NACW's conference. During the opening session, she spoke about her school in Daytona, and Madam C.J. Walker, also in attendance, stepped up to lead a fundraiser for it. This started a friendship and alliance that continued until Walker's death. Walker often donated to the school, and the two women worked together to add Walker's hair-care curriculum to the school's offerings. Before Walker died, she willed a sizable donation to the institute.

Growing dissatisfied with the conservative approach of the NACW, however, Bethune founded the National Council of Negro Women (NCNW) in 1935. As the NCNW president, she eventually spoke for five hundred thousand women, which provided her with political clout without ever having to run for office.

During this time, she became friends with First Lady Eleanor Roosevelt, who asked her to work for the government. President Franklin Roosevelt appointed her director of the Division of Negro Affairs, a role she served in from 1936 to 1944. She created an informal networking group that became known as the "Black Cabinet." They made it possible for black women to enter the Women's Army Corps, which was a women's branch of the United States Army, before they were allowed into the regular army, and for black pilots to be trained in the Civilian Pilot Training Program during World War II.

Along with the NAACP and the Brotherhood of Sleeping Car Porters, which was a union created by black employees of the Pullman Company, the Black Cabinet pushed President Roosevelt to deal with discrimination in defense and government jobs. This resulted in the creation of the Fair Employment Practices Commission. "In spite of the fact that she was never elected to any office, she was probably the most powerful black woman ever to serve in the United States government. So far," said authors Darlene Clark Hine and Kathleen Thompson.[3]

After Roosevelt's death in 1945, Bethune continued to work in the government under President Harry S. Truman. In 1952, she was sent as the official US delegate to the inauguration of Liberian president William Tubman, thus fulfilling a lifelong dream of going to Africa.

A LASTING CONNECTION

Growing hair was one of Walker's biggest claims in her company marketing, but growing connections was something she put a lot of effort into as well. One connection in particular, her friendship with educator Mary McLeod Bethune, stands out as an example of mutual respect and support between friends and leaders.

The two met in 1912 when Walker volunteered to lead a fundraiser for Bethune's Daytona Normal and Industrial Institute, a school for black girls. Over the next seven years, the two became friends, working together in social activism such as the anti-lynching movement. They also supported each other: Walker with donations to the institute and Bethune by adding Walker's curriculum to the school.

When it was clear that Walker's health was failing, she updated her will. Included was a generous bequest of $5,000 (more than $73,000 in 2018) for Bethune's school. Speaking at her institute's commencement, Bethune announced the generous gift and later expressed to Walker via letter how much she and those in the school appreciated the contribution. She added how she hoped that Walker would be spared for the good of humanity; however, Walker died a couple of weeks later.

Bethune's admiration of Walker did not diminish upon her death. "The clearest demonstration I know of Negro woman's ability recorded in history," Bethune said of Walker. "She has gone, but her work still lives and shall live as an inspiration to not only her race but to the world."[4]

"The First Lady of the Struggle," as Mary McLeod Bethune became known, died of a heart attack in 1955, with eleven honorary degrees and affiliations with more than forty organizations. A bronze statue in Lincoln Park, Washington, DC, was dedicated to her in 1974.

Booker T. Washington

Though considered a beloved black leader during difficult times, Booker T. Washington had his critics and left a complicated legacy. Born a slave on a Virginia farm in 1856, he spent half his childhood there. After the Civil War, his mother, Jane, moved them to West Virginia to start a free life with her husband, Washington Ferguson. He worked at the salt furnaces and made his stepsons work with him.

Washington, however, dreamed of learning to read, and his mother helped by giving him a Noah Webster's spelling book. He attended school but had to work before and after. After a few years, he became a houseboy for one of the wealthiest white families in town. The wife was known to be very strict, but he grew to appreciate her, and she allowed him to attend school part time.

At sixteen, he set off on the 500-mile (805 km) journey to the Hampton Institute in Virginia. He was soon at home there, working as a janitor in the school building to pay for what today is the equivalent of a high-school education. He graduated three years later, though the discipline, cleanliness, and order expected by the school's principal, General Samuel Armstrong, would impact his own school later.

The graduate returned home in 1875 and became a teacher. However, he also had other interests. He opened a library, created a debating society, and became involved

Washington speaks at the dedication of a cotton seed mill in the black town of Mound Bayou, Mississippi. Even though he was loved by many, the educator's stance on segregation earned him some detractors.

in politics. In 1879, Armstrong offered him a teaching position at Hampton, and two years later, the general recommended him to run a new school for colored people, the Tuskegee Normal and Industrial Institute, today known as Tuskegee University.

Much of what he learned at Hampton wove its way into the Tuskegee curriculum, with a focus on teaching the trade professions as well as patience, thrift, and cleanliness. Washington believed that financial independence and bettering oneself were the keys for a black person to be accepted by a white community.

Washington is famous for what the school would become under his direction. He knew how to raise funds and talk to both white and black supporters, and he had no issue with taking money from white businessmen to build the school. Over the next thirty-four years, the institute grew to have more than one hundred buildings, 1,500 students, and 200 faculty members. Washington even became an advisor to Presidents Theodore Roosevelt and William Taft.

The year 1895 put Washington squarely in the limelight during the Cotton States and International Exposition in Atlanta, Georgia. He was already a well-known representative of black people. At the exposition, he delivered a speech known as "the Atlanta Compromise." In it, he suggested that freed black people should not seek political power but instead should focus on buying homes and learning trades. He added that they should stay in the South, saying to "cast your bucket where you are."

One part of the speech stated: "Our greatest danger is that in the great leap from slavery to freedom we may overlook the fact that the masses of us are to live by the productions of our hands, and fail to keep in mind that we shall prosper in proportion as we learn to dignify and glorify common labour."[5] In essence, these words suggested that black people of the time should accept many of the restrictions of the Jim Crow laws until they had bettered themselves. White America was eager to accept this compromise, but Jim Crow violence continued. Some black people initially supported Washington. However, over time, many criticized him for not demanding the equality promised in the Fourteenth Amendment.

What the public did not know was that Washington secretly supported several court cases that challenged laws that kept blacks from voting or that segregated public transportation. "As far as the public knew, Washington was true to his public pledge of 1895 not to agitate civil rights … Behind closed doors, however, he was doing just the opposite," said author Raymond W. Smock.[6]

In 1911, he was beaten and arrested in New York City after a white woman claimed that he called her "sweetheart." Though he was released, the trial of the man who beat him, Henry Ulrich, damaged Washington's image. Known for carefully guarding his image and reputation, the trial revealed Washington's motives for being in the neighborhood as unclear. Though the trial slipped from the public eye after Ulrich was also charged with child desertion, Washington's influence in the white supremacist South waned.

It was not long after this incident that Madam C.J. Walker first contacted him. Washington had never considered hairdressers to be important in building black businesses, so he denied her request to attend his farmer's conference in 1912. She persisted, and he relented enough to allow her to speak at a smaller event. Later that year, she would ignore his disregard for her to speak from the floor of his National Negro Business League conference. Eventually, he would realize her potential, asking her for donations and accepting her invitation to be her houseguest when he visited Indianapolis.

When President Woodrow Wilson took office in 1913, it seemed he had little interest in race relations. This meant that Washington's input was not valued by the presidency. As Washington's influence declined, so did his health. In 1915, he was diagnosed with kidney failure and other ailments. He returned home to Tuskegee on November 13 and died less than five hours later.

W. E. B. Du Bois

Known for his philosophical clash with Booker T. Washington and for the African American elite group called the "Talented Tenth," W. E. B. Du Bois was a multifaceted black leader.

The Massachusetts-born teacher, writer, sociologist, and activist came into the world on February 23, 1868. The first to attend high school in his family, William Edward Burghardt Du Bois quickly applied his literacy. At fifteen years old, he began writing articles for papers such as the *Freeman* and the *New York Globe*.

In 1888, he graduated from Tennessee's Fisk University and became the editor of its student magazine. In 1888, he went to Harvard University for advanced degrees in history before starting his PhD at the University of Berlin in Germany. However, his pursuit was cut short when he ran out of funds. He later received his doctorate degree from Harvard while teaching at Wilberforce University in Ohio. There, he met and married his wife, Nina, in 1896.

While teaching at the University of Pennsylvania in 1896, Du Bois dedicated extra time conducting door-to-door interviews for a study of Philadelphia's Seventh Ward. Published as *The Philadelphia Negro* in 1899, it is considered an early example of applying statistics to the field of sociology. His conclusion was that the black community needed to overcome poverty, crime, educational limits, and distrust of noncommunity members.

Based on his work, the US Bureau of Labor Statistics offered him a job that led to more studies on black Southern areas in Virginia, Alabama, and Georgia. These focused on how slavery still affected their lives.

Du Bois's groundbreaking work using statistics and sociology to examine black communities was just the beginning. The man went on to become a founding member of the NAACP and an established leader of the African American community.

It was in *The Philadelphia Negro* that Du Bois began talking of "the Talented Tenth," or the idea that black communities would create leaders if the top 10 percent of blacks were given a classical education and the opportunity to develop intellectual, artistic, or activist pursuits. Based on his research, Du Bois believed that prejudice was a result of the legacy of slavery and of ignorance. If black communities could have more people who were intellectuals and artists, rather than simply focusing on economic prosperity, the black community could integrate more fully into society. "The Talented Tenth rises and pulls all that are worth the saving up to their vantage ground. This is the history of human progress," Du Bois said.[7]

A result of this philosophy and more black migration to the north, the Harlem Renaissance came to life in the 1920s. Many black families moved into the Harlem neighborhood in New York City and created a black pride movement that was promoted by Du Bois. Black writers and artists, including Langston Hughes, Bessie Smith, and Zora Neale Hurston, were drawn to the area and the culture.

After publishing an essay in the *Atlantic Monthly* and his book *The Souls of Black Folk* in 1903, Du Bois became well known. The public saw his more demanding philosophy compared to Booker T. Washington's.

In 1905, Du Bois helped form the Niagara Movement, a civil rights group wanting to bring about great change, as great as the waters of Niagara Falls, near where the group met for the first time. It did not have much success, due to a lack of headquarters and few members, and disbanded in 1910. However, it was a sort of prototype for another organization called the National Association for the Advancement of Color People (NAACP), formed in 1909. Du Bois was one of its founding members. He worked for the NAACP for twenty-four years, as a director and editor of the *Crisis* magazine, which was associated with the organization. During that time, he also continued to publish books.

In 1916, Walker would contribute to the NAACP's anti-lynching fundraising campaign. Soon after, she was invited to a conference for two hundred guests carefully selected by Du Bois. As Walker's activism increased, she and Du Bois crossed paths more often. Both pushed for more black representation at the Paris Peace Conference in 1919.

After World War II, Du Bois became supportive of progressive groups and interested in communism. This led to problems with the NAACP's leadership. He left the organization in 1948.

In 1961, he joined the Communist Party and left the country to live in Ghana. Du Bois focused his attention on completing his *Encyclopedia Africana*, a history collection of those from African descent, but he died in 1963 before it was finished.

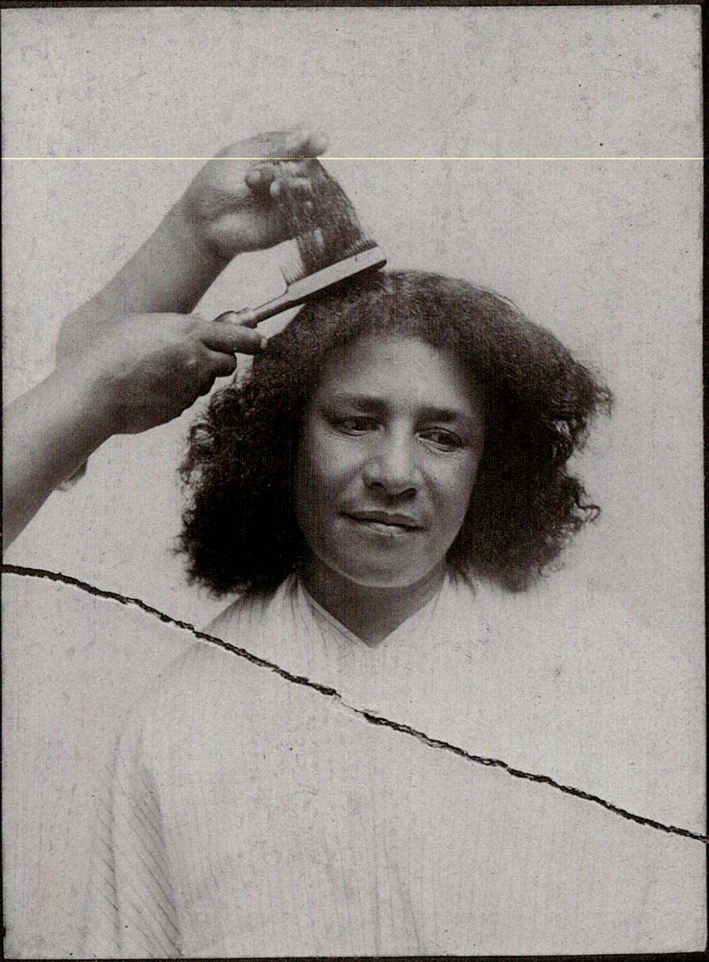

e IV- How to use the comb-
Putting the comb in perfectly straight
not allowing teeth to touch the scalp.

CHAPTER FOUR

The Beauty of Hair and Beyond

Madam C.J. Walker created a hair-care empire from the ground up. Her influence on others as well as on the hair industry helped her become a successful businesswoman. Her key products attracted others and ensured her name was remembered in history.

Wonderful Hair Grower and the Walker System

The formula that Walker claimed came from a dream did more than help heal and grow her own hair. It gave her

Madam C.J. Walker demonstrates how to use the hot comb that was part of her Walker system. This system made her company stand out from the rest.

a first product. The Wonderful Hair Grower, which was used to condition and treat the scalp and to create a healthy shine, was similar to the Poro brand product also called Wonderful Hair Grower. It is likely that the recipes were similar; Walker's great-great-granddaughter A'Lelia Bundles claims the grower was mostly made of petrolatum, sulfur, and beeswax.

Walker started her business with another product: vegetable-based shampoo. These two items used together regularly helped to heal many women's hair, most likely because of the regular hygiene and care required, rather than due to any special ingredients. Walker's customers raved over the results. She also created and sold a dandruff salve, scalp ointment, and glossine, which protected the hair as it was being heat-treated.

With all that Walker achieved in business, what put her on the map was the hair system she developed. "Walker sealed her place in black hair history with the introduction of the Walker system, the 'shampoo-press-and-curl' method of straightening hair that was to become the foundation of the Black beautician industry," said authors Ayana Byrd and Lori Tharps.[1]

When people were properly trained in the Walker system, they received a kit that included a hot comb. This tool was the key to the system. It was a metal comb heated on top of a stove and then pulled through the hair to straighten it until the next shampoo. Walker did not invent this item, though some thought she did. Instead, she repurposed it. The French originally used it in the 1800s to make hair super straight to create the popular hairstyles of the time. Walker was the person to bring it to the attention of black women. She also changed aspects of it. For instance, the comb's teeth were wider, which made it more popular among her customers.

Recruiting a team of trained sales agents helped Walker's business become incredibly successful. It also gave black women a new opportunity to be financially independent. This ad highlights these benefits in an effort to gain more agents.

Walker's method wasn't the only one. Others used tools that Annie Turnbo Malone sold to straighten hair, which were called "pullers." These stretched and straightened the hair. However, Walker believed her hot comb was a gentler option that was better overall for hair.

Given the sensitive politics of hair straightening, Walker often emphasized that she grew hair, not straightened it. Her system using the glossine and a hot comb to smooth hair was what she became known for. It also set her apart from Annie

Turnbo Malone and other competitors. Without the Walker system's success, it's likely that her business success and the opening of the Lelia College, a beauty school, would not have been possible.

Growing a Business

In 1908, just a couple years after becoming an entrepreneur, Walker settled her business in Pittsburgh, Pennsylvania. Despite the economy suffering from a national banking crisis, she opened a hair parlor in the city. Soon she would found the Lelia College, named for her daughter, where she and other teachers would train more "hair culturists" to take her system and products to new markets. These sales agents would sell to customers in areas Walker's company was underserving. This tactic had multiple benefits. It not only increased the visibility of Walker's company and her products, but it also enabled Walker to recruit more women—these new customers—to be sales agents. Agents were motivated by gifts and monetary incentives, which Walker provided. Today called multilevel marketing, or pyramid marketing, this built the company in a short time.

Just as the Walker system made the college possible, the college and multilevel structure made Walker's next step possible: bringing small groups of agents together and forming clubs as part of the Madam C.J. Walker Benevolent Association. The association was part of Walker's plan to pull her agents together to further social and political goals. The purpose of the agent clubs was to show the agents how to boost their sales and to encourage them to give to charitable causes. To help bring these clubs together, Walker spent several months on the road in 1916. While there, she recruited new agents. To enable some of the poorer women in the South to join, and thus increase her numbers of agents, she lowered the price of training classes by more than half.

An Agents' Convention

Before long, Walker had more than ten thousand sales agents. It was at that time that she prepared to make a dream into a reality: to host a national gathering of Walker sales agents. In August 1917, approximately two hundred agents attended the Madam C.J. Walker Hair Culturists Union of America Convention in Philadelphia. With badges announcing themselves as attendees of the event, the women enjoyed business sessions and speakers. They also shared personal stories of how working as an agent had changed their lives. For her own speech, Walker shared that while the standards of the company were high, she wanted to work closely with her agents and share in the profits.

She also took advantage of the convention to again encourage others in the black community to work to make their neighborhoods and country a better place. She promoted both charity and activism. "After all, this is the greatest country under the sun. But we must not let our love of country, our patriotic loyalty cause us to abate one whit in our protest against wrong and injustice."[2]

At the end of the event, the new union sent a telegram to President Woodrow Wilson, who was not acting against the lynching of black people or a race riot in Saint Louis. Their unified protest read:

> We respectfully submit to you this our protest against the continuation of such wrongs and injustices in this "land of the free, and home of the

> brave" and we further respectfully urge that you as President of these United States use your great influence that Congress enact the necessary laws to prevent a recurrence of such disgraceful affairs.[3]

From selling hair grower door-to-door to organizing a national event, Walker proved that she had truly arrived as a leader and businesswoman. She did not just fulfill a desire for a better life. She extended that dream to thousands of other black women and inspired them to pay it forward, as she had.

A Giver's Heart and an Activist's Spirit

Someone once requested a list of Walker's charitable efforts. Her lawyer wrote one three pages long, adding that it wasn't a complete list. Clearly, Madam Walker learned to wield her influence to help others in spite of the limits society tried to put on her.

"While she was still black, female, and subject to the larger structures of Jim Crow America," said Tyrone Freeman, professor of philanthropic studies, "Walker's growing wealth and potential provided just enough insulation and options to enable her to dream even bigger dreams than Sarah had … Madam Walker's dreams included … engaging a type of philanthropic giving that called upon every available resource at her disposal to uplift the race and make life better for others."[4]

It didn't hurt that she also had good people helping her run the business, including F.B. Ransom, the lawyer and business manager that made the list. Building a foundation of dedicated employees and working hard gave her the opportunity to dig deeper into activism and philanthropy.

Advertising with positive messages was one way that Walker tried to make black women feel better. The entrepreneur always kept the uplift of black people at the forefront of her business.

One of the first nonchurch groups that Walker became part of was the National Association for Colored Women (NACW). She met several members through her church in Saint Louis while she worked as a washerwoman. Little did she know that in less than ten years' time, she would be one of the group's leading voices.

Created when two other groups merged in 1896, the NACW encouraged self-help among black women. In 1916, there were hundreds of NACW clubs in the country and almost one hundred thousand members. The NACW believed that by lifting up black women, it would also help black men and children. With Walker's emphasis on helping women, it isn't hard to assume that she agreed with this view. The group was also active with anti-lynching campaigns, which was another cause that Walker championed.

When she moved to Denver and married C.J. Walker, she was able to move further into the social circles of the NACW. Over the years, she became more active, and the structure of the NACW inspired many of Walker's own decisions later when building her business and clubs. While this organization was not the one she put most of her energy into, it was the one that likely most affected her outlook and business organization.

With a wider social circle and inspiring connections in organizations, Walker started making donations focused on helping build up the black community. Her philanthropic gifts that got the most notice early on were made to the colored Young Men's Christian Association (YMCA) in Indianapolis, Indiana, after she had moved there. At the time, the YMCA was much more than a gym. People could stay there in safe dorm-like rooms when visiting or if they were between homes. The Y also offered opportunities for getting vocational training, education, and recreational activities.

African Americans at the time viewed the YMCA (and the YWCA) as a way to help their people and as a source of pride in their communities. Soon after Walker had moved to Indianapolis, Indiana, the black leaders there began fundraising to build a black YMCA facility. During a fundraising campaign in October 1911, Walker started the event with a pledge of $1,000 (over $26,600 in 2018). At the time, she was making about that much every month, so it was a huge donation. "By making her $1,000 YMCA gift pledge—which almost equaled the total gifts and pledges made by 99 other donors—and subsequent smaller and more regular donations to local, national, and international black YMCAs, Madam Walker expressed the value she placed on the YMCA as a vehicle for uplifting the race and overcoming prejudice," said Tyrone Freeman, assistant professor at Indiana University.[5]

The black press claimed she was the first black woman to give that much to a black YMCA, and others questioned if a black woman could truly afford to pay that $1,000 pledge. She did honor that pledge and helped lead the black community to donate beyond the target amount. In the next decade, she would continue to give to this YMCA and ones in Saint Louis and New York. She said the Saint Louis gift was in honor of the help she received there in raising her daughter. New York became her future home and was also a place she focused her generosity. However, this first large donation brought her national media attention and also built a relationship with George Knox, who led the Indianapolis fundraiser. "During an era when African Americans were believed to be incapable of developing their own communities, she had refuted the

UNTIL BUSINESS DO US PART

Marriage was not something that went well for Walker, considering her first husband died when she was twenty and her second husband had been more trouble than he was worth. Yet her third marriage to Charles Joseph Walker, called C.J., was a pivotal point in her life. It helped Sarah Breedlove become Madam C.J. Walker, the name history would know her by. Their union gave her a new identity and was the beginning of her own personal uplift.

She began dating the well-dressed man in 1902 or 1903. He was charming but a bit of a boaster and had some formal education. When Breedlove left Saint Louis to sell Poro products in Denver, Colorado, he soon joined her. They married shortly after that, and they both dug into their own business ventures. Though they each later took credit for the idea of starting the Walker Manufacturing business, it is clear that they both traveled together extensively to build the company. Seeing the success of her products, C.J. attempted to add a few of his own. He developed and sold several medicines for sores and rheumatism, but they never sold as well as Walker's hair products.

As the company grew, the couple started traveling separately to cover more ground, or so Madam Walker could handle the home base. As they worked to increase sales nationally, their relationship was falling apart. Madam Walker's great-great-granddaughter explained some of the tensions between them. "The more they were together, especially in the company of others," she said, "the clearer it became that Madam Walker was the more impressive member of the couple and the more effective entrepreneur."[6]

C.J. had an eye for clothes and cars, which led him to waste company money. He also had affairs with other women. When C.J. and one of these women conspired to start a competing business, Madam Walker found out and filed divorce papers. C.J. did not appear in court, and the divorce was done without drama. From that point on, Walker was the sole driving force of the business—even her daughter Lelia did not have the passion and instinct for the business that she did.

Though she was likely embarrassed by C.J.'s actions, he pushed her to become a smart and capable business leader because of the hopes and dreams they shared during their relationship.

stereotype that blacks could not be successful in business," said A'Lelia Bundles.[7] But there was more to the Indianapolis gift than getting attention and respect. In her will, she left the facility money, even though she had only lived there for five years. The city had provided solid ground for building her business, and she was always thankful for that.

An organization that Walker supported generously in her later years was the NAACP. Started in 1910, it was still a fledgling group when its organizers approached her for a donation to their anti-lynching efforts in 1916 after she moved to New York. She received many flattering headlines from the local papers, and the *New York News* said she had "risen to command the respect of tens of thousands of both races."[8] Combined with her known interest in causes at the national level, the NAACP was smart to view her as a future supporter.

She and NAACP director W. E. B. Du Bois knew of one another before that, however. Du Bois had run an article in the group's newsletter, the *Crisis,* about her Indianapolis YMCA pledge and other projects years earlier. In return, she had advertised in the *Crisis.* Du Bois counted her among the select two hundred guests invited to the 1916 Amenia Conference to discuss the rights of black people. Though there was not much correspondence between the two, they would continue to cross paths as activists for the black community.

It was clear Walker meant a lot to the NAACP, and the NAACP meant a lot to Walker. Its first board chairman responded to her initial $100 donation to the organization's anti-lynching fundraiser personally, showing just how much the organization valued her. Soon after, the group invited her to the 1916 Amenia Conference, but she could not attend due to travel plans. Walker continued to support the group and its efforts, especially its involvement with the anti-lynching

Madam C.J. Walker donated regularly to the NAACP in life and again in her will.

movement, until her death. On her deathbed, she left them $4,000 (over $58,000 in 2018) in her will, the fifth-largest charity gift in the document.

Walker's intentions and actions in activism did not always turn out well. For example, she helped create the International League of Darker Peoples (ILDP) in 1919. This group strove to protest the European countries that were scrambling to colonize African lands. The ILDP also wanted to bring attention to the struggle for freedom by African Americans and other people of color around the world, including Asian people. The group hoped to have an impact on the Paris Peace Conference that was gathering world leaders. As she did with other groups, she would offer her home as a meeting place. Walker's lawyer, F.B. Ransom, believed this group was too socialist and too open on the subject of immigration. He feared being part of the group would hurt Walker's name and business, but he also thought most blacks should focus on the NAACP instead of spreading their efforts far and wide. He noted his dislike of her involvement in a letter. "I have not written you on this matter before today because I have been trying to wait until I could write you calmly," he began before saying she needed to be careful not to let her home be used by "theorists, propagandists, etc."[9]

Walker gave in to her lawyer's wishes, though she wanted to continue with the ILDP. As it turns out, Ransom was correct. Due to her involvement with the group, army intelligence began to monitor her activity. Later, she was denied a passport to attend the Paris Peace Conference after World War I.

Of course, Walker's charity and activism went far beyond these three organizations. She also supported the Colored Orphan Home of Saint Louis and the Colored Alpha Home, a nursing home for black women. Several schools benefited from her money and visible support, especially the Tuskegee Institute and the Daytona Normal and Industrial Institute. During World War I, she worked within the Circle for Negro War Relief to help black soldiers. The effect of her asking her sales agents to give back as she had cannot be measured.

In life, she had hoped to leave two-thirds of her fortune to charity and to the upkeep of Villa Lewaro. Upon her death,

One of Madam Walker's crowning achievements was building her New York home, Villa Lewaro. She designed the estate to be a meeting place as well as her home.

only approximately 10 percent of her estate went to charity. After her estate's debts and obligations had been met, there wasn't as much money left as she might have hoped. Her health had deteriorated quickly in her last years, and she had only lived to the age of fifty-one. It's possible that she would have left things in a better place if she had had more time to do so.

CHAPTER FIVE

Gaining Independence and Sharing Empowerment

Madam C.J. Walker did not set out to become a businesswoman. She set out to heal her own hair and scalp. She believed that doing so would improve her chances of moving up socially and getting a better job. This was important because she realized she could not do the hard work of a laundress when she was older. She was simply seeking a more secure future for herself and her daughter. Her flowering into a business tycoon was due to luck, timing, and determination.

For many slaves, the head rag was a part of life. Many black women, like Walker, continued to suffer from scalp diseases and hair loss long after slavery ended.

Helping Herself

During slavery, women did not have the time to devote to hair grooming that they'd had in their African homeland. Lice and ringworm infections would spread among slaves who lived in close quarters. These diseases, along with other poor conditions, caused patchy hair growth and even baldness to occur in some people. To cover infected scalps, slave women wore scarves or head rags over their hair: "Partly as protection from the scorching sun and hovering flies and partly out of shame for the now unsightly hair, the head rag became ubiquitous in slave culture."[1]

Many black women who lived in the decades after the Civil War suffered from the same scalp and hair problems. Walker was born into this era and grew up poor; she had to work hard from a very early age. She picked cotton with her family as a small child, was orphaned at seven years old, and was put to work as a laundress by her brother-in-law soon after. A widow at twenty, she worked hard to scrape by. Her hair suffered the normal consequences, and she had short, patchy hair.

She spent several years of her life working as a laundress, and historian Carter G. Woodson noted that the black washerwomen were often the foundation of their communities. They were usually the primary earners in their homes, as many black men were kept out of unions and other good jobs. The laundresses often bought homes, paid for their children's schooling, and helped to fund new businesses. "Washerwomen, according to Woodson, regularly gave money to help the less-fortunate despite their own great need … for Woodson, the black washerwoman's sacrificial toil and unbounded generosity made her the quintessential philanthropist among African Americans," said Tyrone Freeman.[2]

Starting so young in the career, Walker would have been exposed to women who personified this ideal. This could have inspired much of her desire to help organize women, support her community, and be generous.

After she moved to Saint Louis, she joined the Saint Paul African Methodist Episcopal (AME) Church. There, she met several respected women, many of whom were active in community organizations: "Through the AME Church, Sarah, and later Madam Walker, was exposed to an ambitious, visionary, action-oriented institution that was created, funded, and managed by blacks during a time when American society on the whole made little room for them."[3]

With the influence of both the washerwomen and her church, it is easy to see how Walker would later so easily connect her business efforts with work to help black people overcome the barriers laid at their feet by society.

While working as a washerwoman in Saint Louis, Walker also saw an NACW address by Margaret Murray Washington, educator, activist, and wife of Booker T. Washington, and was impressed by how she looked as well as her message. It clicked for her that being physically appealing added to one's impact on others. She believed that fixing her hair would be a step toward improving her appearance and her opportunities in life. She began a search for products to help her hair and eventually found Annie Turnbo Malone's line of Poro products. This, in turn, led her to form the Walker Manufacturing Company.

Overcoming racial discrimination was only half of Walker's battle to become a respected businesswoman. In a white-dominated society and a male-dominated society, black women were at the bottom no matter how you looked at it. "Black women were subjected to the oppression, indifference, and hostility of not only white men and black men, but also white women," said Tyrone Freeman.[4] Businesses like Walker's had the unusual advantage of being for black women by black women. Over and over, the entrepreneur pointed out that she wanted to help other black women. Though she spent her money helping all black people in the best ways she knew how, her business focused on helping women specifically.

Though it was not a perfect company and there were sales agents who were dissatisfied with how things ran, there were also many testimonies by Walker employees who stated that working for Walker changed their lives. One Florida sales agent wrote: "I have all I can do at home and don't have to go

Many of Walker's sales agents appreciated the opportunity to earn a living within their own black communities. Walker stressed pride in being black and making clients feel beautiful inside and out.

out and work for White people in kitchens and factories."[5] Many of her agents earned well over the average salary for a more traditional workingwoman's job, such as a cook or a laundress.

While Walker enjoyed her money with shopping sprees and a lavish home, she also enjoyed seeing other women given opportunities through her business. To the National Negro Business League convention in 1914, she said:

> I am not merely satisfied in making money for myself, for I am endeavoring to provide employment for hundreds of the women of my race. I had little or no opportunity when I started out in life, having been left an orphan ... I had to make my own living and my own opportunity! But I made it! That is why I want to say to every Negro woman present, don't sit down and wait for the opportunities to come ... Get up and make them![6]

She made her own opportunities, though she was lucky to have many talented people alongside her—C.J., who was familiar with advertising, and Lelia, who was willing to help her build the business. Likewise, she was also fortunate to have been born at a time when black people were first experiencing a middle-class lifestyle. These elements, infused with the ambition and eagerness to contribute gained through her earlier occupation and her church, created a legend with a legacy.

Sharing the Faith

Being a Walker sales agent and convincing women that the brand was best for them was more than a sales pitch. It was giving a testimony of faith in the Walker products. When women bought Walker's Wonderful Hair Grower or luster products, they were buying more than an ointment or oil. They were also putting faith in the products.

This faith was important to Walker's success because her products, in truth, were not original. They were very similar to her competitors', such as those of her former employer, Annie Turnbo Malone. Much of what helped grow the hair of African American women was teaching them maintenance techniques like regularly shampooing, massaging the scalp, eating better, and using sulfur-based products, which was similar to other hair shampoos at the time. What Walker and her agents were really selling was self-care, Walker's personal story, and a belief that the Walker products would work.

Because Walker's story was infused into the idea of her products, each agent became a surrogate of Walker herself. In an era before television, each agent was a loudspeaker through which Walker spread her message, an advertiser, and a champion of her company.

It is important to remember that Walker's inspiring story came at a time when society was often hostile and cruel to black people. The way they were treated and discriminated against suggested that many whites thought little of their humanity and value to society. In such a world, here came Walker and her personal story of determination, financial success, and generosity.[7]

Walker became a symbol of personal achievement and empowerment for her agents. She was able to propel herself forward without siding with either Booker T. Washington's or W. E. B. Du Bois's philosophical debates. "She and her agents were able to gain economic mobility by selling the hair-care products that enforced respectable presentation of

While living through a time of discrimination and violence, Walker built a successful company. Though segregation continued for decades after her death, Walker helped start the fight that would lead to the civil rights movement.

black femininity," said Indiana University graduate student Aaron Coombs.[8] She would find ways to work with anyone she believed would help improve black people's chances in life.

One way she built her business and capitalized on opportunities to help others through it was by weaving elements of her Christian faith into her company ethos. The concepts of charity and of giving others a helping hand were chief among them. Many of Madam Walker's special touches emphasized the spiritual aspect of her company's message. For instance, she often held her speaking events at churches. Her sales agent clubs started meetings with the "Hairdressers' Ode to Madam C.J. Walker Agents." This song was set to the tune of the popular gospel song, "Onward Christian Soldiers." The tune would have been familiar to most of the members and linked a sense of triumph to the cause. Meanwhile, the lyrics reinforced company principles of cleanliness and making customers feel good about themselves:

> Onward, Walker Hair Dressers,
> Outward to the fray;
> Have your combs all sterilized,
> Keep a shining tray …
> Think forever of the one
> In whose name we stand;
> Keep the honor that she won,
> The best one in the land.
> Treat your client courteous,
> Always pleasant be;
> Let your smiles and patience
> Last eternally.[9]

Words such as "fray," which referred to the struggle for equal rights, also aligned the company with the efforts of racial uplift. This was important to Walker's personal work in charity and activism, as well as how she marketed her business. Her sales agents were instructed to learn Walker's story so they could use some part of it to help potential customers personally connect to the company. "Imagine yourself a missionary and convert him," they were instructed.[10]

In later years, Walker incorporated a multimedia element to her speeches, making them "illustrated lectures." With glass slides in a Stereopticon projector, an early slide projector that was fairly new technology at the time, she included images of her personal journey, such as a sharecropper's cabin, washtubs, and her cars. Using this media format increased the appeal of her lectures.

Through these methods, the entrepreneur created a community for her beauty products and her message of financial independence and self-esteem. In fact, when looking at her spiritual emphasis, her use of the media available, and her focus on bettering others, it is easy to compare her to a well-known woman today: media tycoon Oprah Winfrey.

Some today view Walker as a precursor or inspiration for Winfrey and how she encourages self-improvement through public confession and "rapport talk" on her talk show and magazine. Much like how Walker shared her life of hard labor and embarrassing hair loss, Winfrey has shared her struggles with her weight, sexual abuse, and more to connect with her talk-show guests and to help them open up on national television. Winfrey's style includes spiritual aspects as well. "Oprah revolutionized television by invoking the language and performed rituals of spiritualization in order to address, celebrate, and inspire personal achievement," said Coombs.[11]

Like Walker, Winfrey has tapped into her popularity to lend support to charities, social causes, and politics. She focuses much energy on causes that support families, children, human rights, and preventing abuse. Politically, her endorsement of President Barack Obama during his 2008 presidential campaign made headlines. Some have even proposed that Winfrey herself should make a bid for the White House. Both Walker and Winfrey built their brand around helping others.

Media mogul Oprah Winfrey exemplifies many of the traits that made Madam C.J. Walker successful. They both prove that personal connection is a powerful tool.

More than Good Hair

During slavery, often lighter-skinned slaves with hair that didn't kink or frizz came to be known as people with "good hair." These slaves often got the better positions in the household, while darker slaves with kinkier hair worked in the fields or other demanding jobs. "Black people themselves internalized the concept and within their own ranks propagated the notion that darker-skinned Blacks with kinkier hair were less attractive, less intelligent, and worth less than their lighter hued brothers and sisters," according to the authors of *Hair Story: Untangling the Roots of Black Hair in America.*[12]

The concepts of "good hair" and "lighter is better" continued within black society well after the Civil War. It even separated black people among themselves, with some black organizations and churches requiring their members to be in the lighter range of black. Some black leaders highlighted this self-loathing of their darkness and naturally kinky hair as something that needed to change.

As such, when Walker and her competitors had booming businesses, the beauty ideal of straight hair that some of their products enabled did not always go over well. Some black leaders, including Booker T. Washington, preached against hair straightening. They believed it was wasting time and money on "getting white." They wanted black people to focus on getting better rather than trying to look whiter. Some today look back at these entrepreneurs and feel they should have promoted natural hairstyles more.

Even W. E. B. Du Bois supported this idea of having pride in one's blackness. It is interesting to note, however, that he and many of those in his "Talented Tenth" met the "good

RECLAIMING A HAIR TRADITION

Walker and her competitors blazed a trail to create new opportunities for black women in the United States. At the same time, they were reclaiming a heritage of hair care from black barbers and hairdressers.

Not all blacks in the country were slaves before the Civil War. By the beginning of the 1800s, there were more than one hundred thousand free blacks in the country. They worked in a variety of jobs, as lawyers, teachers, and bankers. A good business for blacks, in both the North and the South, was to own a barbershop that catered to white clientele. To the well-off whites, they provided pampering with spas, beauty treatments, barbers, and hairdressers.

In the decades leading up to the Civil War, and then again in the Jim Crow era, black men were maligned as violent in the South. As a result, many of the Southern hair businesses catering to whites closed. Some black women were able to fill in this service instead. Even the legendary Voodoo Queen of New Orleans, Marie Laveau, reportedly worked as a hairdresser for wealthy white women.

As the nineteenth century began, the black middle class had more money to spend on things that weren't needs. Hair services and products were among the things they would buy. White manufacturers made most of the products available to African Americans at that time. These products didn't sell well, though, due to poor marketing and mediocre performance by the product.

This left the door open for manufacturers such as Walker and Annie Turnbo Malone, who knew how to target and advertise to their own race. They quickly took a large percentage of the market. Their desire to help black communities and to make black women feel better about themselves helped bring their companies much success and were an integral part of their business philosophies.

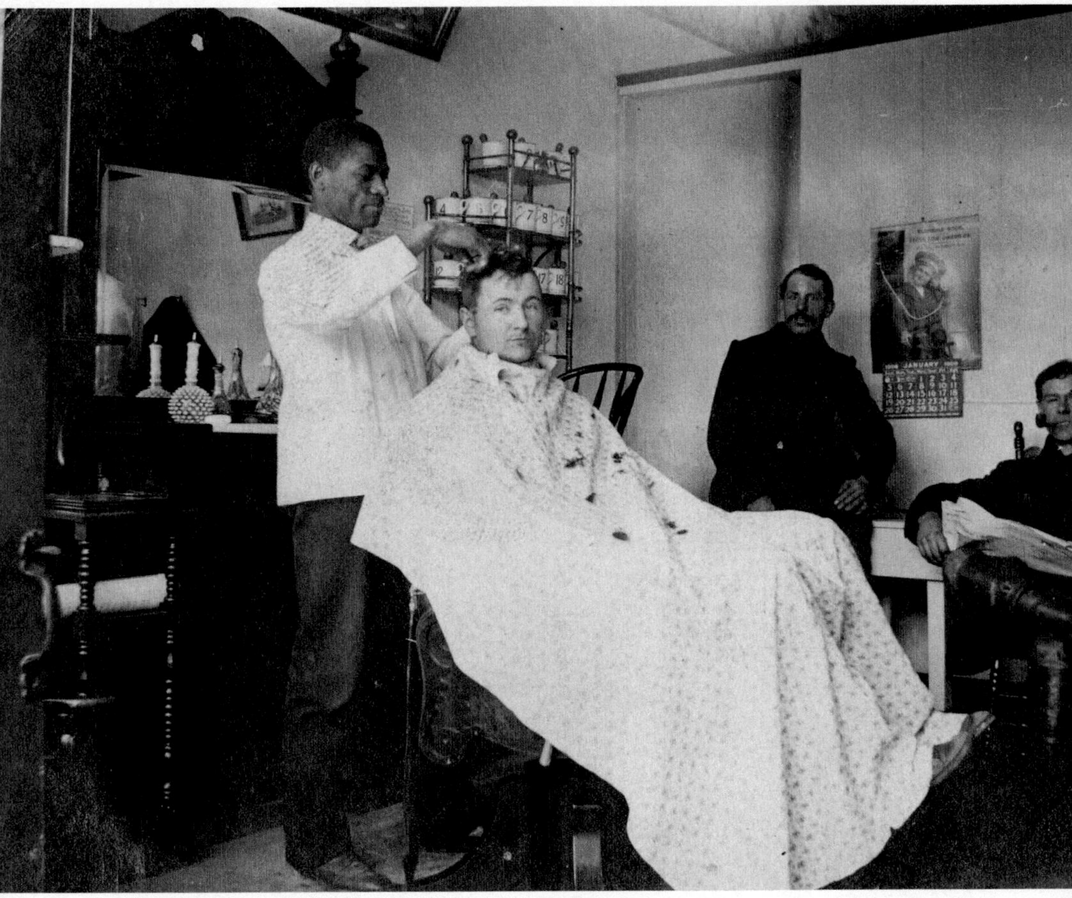

For many years, including before slavery ended, free black people served as barbers and hairdressers for wealthy white people. This barber cuts the hair of a man in 1908.

This group photo of students at Roger Williams University in Tennessee shows the difference in skin tones and hair textures among black people. The idea that lighter-skinned and straighter-haired black people were somehow "better" has roots in slavery.

hair" standard that had helped elevate blacks in white society for generations.

Ayana Byrd and Lori Tharps, authors of *Hair Story: Untangling the Roots of Black Hair in America*, believe that's an unfair view. Walker, Malone, and others did not create the beauty ideal of straight hair for blacks, but they offered an option different from the products made by white manufacturers. "Instead they sought to create safe, affordable products that would give all classes of Black women the means of achieving this straight-haired ideal," Byrd and Tharps write.

"Walker emphasized to her agents that they should pamper their clients so they felt beautiful inside and out."[13]

Even Washington would come to accept Walker, despite his early misgivings about her business. Her ability to do good and influence change was hard to miss, regardless of philosophical differences. Walker simply sought to make black women feel good about themselves, just like she had felt after conquering her own hair problems.

What's more important than how leaders such as Washington viewed Walker is how the public did. Many loved her presentations and clamored for her products and a chance at the same rags-to-riches rise that Walker had achieved. She worked to make black women feel better about themselves and, unlike her competitor Malone, had a personality that drew people to her. She was extroverted and outgoing. Malone, though she had many loyal customers and was also a generous giver, had a more reserved personality.

WALKER
THEATRE

CHAPTER SIX

A Thriving Legacy

Dynamic personality that she was, Madam C.J. Walker made a lasting impression. Her wealth enabled her to create opportunities and jobs as well as to construct impressive buildings and give generously.

A Direct Legacy

Some of the things that Madam C.J. Walker gave to the world are easy to spot. She used a portion of her fortune to create lasting landmarks. Some of it she used to help others, which made her a lasting figure in the black community. Two of the most obvious signs of Walker's legacy are the places her money built. These are her lavish

The Madam C.J. Walker Theatre Center in Indianapolis is one of several lasting legacies of Walker's drive and passion for community building.

home Villa Lewaro in New York and the Madam C.J. Walker Theatre Center in Indianapolis, Indiana.

Villa Lewaro was maintained by a trust through the Walker estate for years after Walker's death. With the stock market crash of 1929, however, the trustees didn't have the money to continue caring for the property. In 1930, they auctioned the contents. The home was supposed to have been given to the NAACP after Lelia's death in 1931, but the organization declined the offer, as they couldn't afford its upkeep during the Great Depression. Villa Lewaro was sold to a women's organization in 1932, and it was designated as a National Historic Landmark in 1976. It was bought and refurbished by Harold Doley and his wife in 1993. In 2017, the Doleys began working with the National Trust to find a way to turn the property into a museum. In the future, the mansion could help educate the public about Walker and the Villa's architect, Vertner Woodson Tandy.

The building of the Madam C.J. Walker Theatre Center was actually completed by Walker's daughter in 1927. It was the company's new headquarters and manufacturing building and was a center of activity for thirty years. In the 1950s, the whole area declined, and the building was not well cared for. In 1970, preservation efforts helped save it. The center was declared a National Historic Landmark. In 2018, the theater and Indiana University partnered to start a $15 million renovation of the building and to make it more useful to the community. The partners worked with the community to determine what programs and changes would be most beneficial.

Recognition of Walker's work has come from national organizations too. First, she was inducted into the National Women's Hall of Fame in 1993, where she is listed along with women such as Susan B. Anthony and Maya Angelou. Five

In 1998, Walker's great-great-granddaughter A'Lelia Bundles (*fourth from right*) helped reveal a Black Heritage stamp featuring Walker. Walker's family has been instrumental in keeping the entrepreneur's memory alive.

years later, in 1998, she appeared on a United States postage stamp as part of a Black Heritage series.

The success of Walker's legacy is largely due to a descendant's inheritance of Walker's tenacious streak. In 2001, Walker's great-great-granddaughter, A'Lelia Bundles, published an in-depth biography of her famous ancestor. Explaining the history behind the events of Walker's life, the book has become popular for Walker fans and researchers.

Bundles has also donated family items to museums and lobbied for her ancestor's recognition. She helps run Walker's Legacy, an organization to empower women in business. Its nonprofit branch, Walker's Legacy Foundation, is inspired by Walker's giving nature. It aims to improve the lives and financial education of low-income, multicultural women and girls. Its programs provide training in leadership, business, technology, and public speaking for ages twelve and up.

Now, Bundles's biography of Walker might soon be coming into homes all over. In 2018, streaming service Netflix gave the green light to create a television series about the entrepreneur. Oscar-winning actress Octavia Spencer is set

Walker's legacy is receiving star treatment: Oscar-winning actress Octavia Spencer will portray her in a television series about the entrepreneur.

to executive-produce as well as taking on the role of Walker. The show, in production and slated for a 2019 release, will only expand her legend and continue to encourage people to overcome barriers to reach their goals.

A Civil Rights Legacy

Sometimes the effect a person has on the world continues in unexpected ways. When thinking about the civil rights movement of the 1950s and 1960s, it might be hard to see what Madam C.J. Walker would have to do with it. After all, it started more than thirty years after she died. What many do not know about this civil rights movement is that beauticians played an important part in it. Beauty salons became centers of communication for those who fought for civil rights. Some beauticians helped blacks through the process of registering to vote in states that tried to prevent it. The Highlander Folk School in Tennessee taught beauticians about civil disobedience and voter registration, in addition to beauty treatments. These ladies funded some civil rights efforts, such as helping to rent buses and to support civil rights leaders who had lost their jobs. One example was Bernice Robinson of South Carolina. She was known to help someone through the process of registering to vote while giving a customer a shampoo. She even encouraged other salon owners to host citizen education classes.

So how could they do this without being the target of white supremacists? These businesses served black customers and were not controlled by whites, so no one had to worry about losing their jobs. More importantly, they were under the radar. White supremacists that tried to intimidate civil rights leaders throughout the 1950s and 1960s did not view beauty salons as a threat, so they didn't bother monitoring those locations. "And that's really where I think a lot of the power of these institutions came from, the fact that they were seen as frivolous," said professor of history Tiffany Gill.[1] This was a serious mistake.

Walker frequently mixed business with politics, and her company trained thousands of sales agents and created its own beautician curriculum. By the 1950s, curricula for beauty colleges mirrored much of what Walker had trained her agents

Sit-ins, such as this one at an Oklahoma restaurant in 1958, were a well-known element of the civil rights movement. Less known is that beauty salons supported and even funded the movement.

to do. This included how to talk about politics and causes with clients. Plus, Walker's training and clubs had a high level of organization, which also helped, as beauticians could pass on messages, planning, and helping with civil rights events.

A Legacy Reborn

Some would say that Walker's legacy does not affect black women much today. After all, part of Walker's money came from products that were designed to help black women have smoother, straighter hair. Today, African American women (and men) have many styling options that are considered professional and fashionable—twist outs, angled or long afros, Bantu knots, braids, dreadlocks, curly, or straightened. While the media sometimes singles out black celebrities for either embracing natural hair or straight hair, overall, there are more choices today.

Walker herself always wanted women to feel good about themselves—inside and out—not just to sell a specific hairstyle. It isn't hard to imagine how excited she might have been to see the variety of hairstyles that have become popular today. Further, she helped create the atmosphere of the modern hair salon through her company's salons. The Walker salons and agents provided black women specialized areas and opportunities that supported them. Many salons today continue that legacy, including ones that share health information with clients while working on hair.

Many of Walker's advertising and business strategies continue to work well today. In addition to providing a positive approach to advertising, Walker's life story became a huge part of her sales pitch. It made others connect to her on a personal level too. Today, companies employ this same idea to

WALKER'S PHILANTHROPY

Walker has sometimes been overlooked for her charitable giving. However, like her early mentor and competitor Annie Turnbo Malone, Walker gave away thousands during her lifetime and willed two-thirds of her income to the upkeep of her home and to charity upon her death. She gave $25,000 (over $365,400 in 2018) to Howard University in Washington, DC, for its medical program, and gave much to the YMCAs in several cities, the NAACP, and more. She also focused her spending on black-owned businesses to further benefit the black community.

Some say that Walker and other businesspeople like her were lost in the shadow of white philanthropic giants like Andrew Carnegie and John D. Rockefeller, causing historians to overlook her and the others. Rockefeller gave more than $500 million ($8.3 billion in 2018) to different causes, while Carnegie gave more than $350 million ($5.1 billion in 2018). The key difference, of course, is that the two men also made vastly more money than Walker, Malone, and the majority of entrepreneurs of the time. By comparison, at her death Walker was not yet a millionaire, with an estimated estate value of $600,000 ($8.7 million in 2018) and her company worth approximately $1 million ($14.6 million in 2018).

Even though she had met Carnegie and knew the large donations both he and Rockefeller had made to the Tuskegee Institute, she also knew another key difference between men like them and herself. "I am unlike your white friends who have waited until they were rich and then help," she wrote to Booker T. Washington in reply to his asking her for more donations.[2] She continued to explain that she had given in proportion to her wealth though she had frequent requests for more donations because she was well known. Walker knew that she had done what she could for others even when she was earning just a few dollars a week as a laundress.

Serving clients with a smile was important to Madam C.J. Walker, as was providing safe products for their use. Here, Walker agents work the cosmetics desk at a Madam C.J. Walker Beauty Shoppe.

help customers relate to them—in their ads, on their company websites, and in newsletters and other correspondence. A personal touch also shows customers that the company truly wants to provide quality products or services. Walker's use of "we" and "our" instead of "I" and "my" in flyers and letters sent to sales agents helped make the company about the team of agents and not just about her. This tactic is still commonly used today to make communication more engaging and inclusive to the readers.

Another way Walker affects hair and culture today is with the products still made in her name. In 2016, beauty companies Sundial Brands and Sephora launched the Madam C.J. Walker Beauty Culture brand. This lineup includes items for different hair types and styles, and emphasizes cleaning and treating hair as well as styling it—something Walker would have approved.

It was a timely restart to Walker products. Research showed that black hair-care products were selling more, yet the sales of relaxers used to straighten hair were going down. The CEO of Sundial Brands, Richelieu Dennis, said Walker's story still means a lot to people. This is what pushed Sundial to create the new line. He said, "I felt it wasn't right that the most relevant and cultural icon of beauty and the beauty business, and the representation of what beauty means to our community, was not represented the same ways as Estée Lauder and Coco Chanel."[3]

Bundles was excited that the legacy continued with this new line. "Part of what I like about his collection is, there is something for every texture: locks, curly-kinky, wavy and heat-treated … Now a younger generation is teaching all of us something about letting your hair speak for itself."[4]

Regardless of how her legacy is viewed today, Walker made an impact on the lives of thousands of women in just a decade. Not only did she help black women feel better about themselves, but she also convinced thousands of them to join her in business. She was a vibrant woman with a big personality who used her influence to help uplift the black community in the early twentieth century.

CHRONOLOGY

1867 Sarah Breedlove (later Madam C.J. Walker) is born.

1875 Walker is orphaned and goes to live with her sister.

1881 or 1882 Marries Moses McWilliams at age fourteen.

1885 Gives birth to her daughter, Lelia.

1888 Moses dies.

1889 She and Lelia move to Saint Louis, Missouri, to be with family.

1894 Marries John Davis.

1903 Fixes her own hair and becomes a Poro sales agent after separating from John Davis. Later, she begins seeing C.J. Walker.

1905 Moves to Denver, Colorado, to sell Poro products.

1906 Develops her own line of products.

1908 Moves her business to Pittsburgh, Pennsylvania, and opens a hair parlor.

1910 Creates a new company headquarters in Indianapolis, Indiana.

1911 In October, pledges $1,000 to the Indianapolis YMCA and is featured in the NAACP's the *Crisis* for it.

1912 Divorces C.J. Walker. Attends the National Negro Business League and speaks from the floor of the gathering when she is snubbed by Booker T. Washington.

1913 Invites Washington to be her houseguest during the YMCA building opening.

1916 Moves to New York after building her company over several years and is approached by the NAACP for a donation and later invited to their conference. She becomes ill while traveling for work and takes a six-week break in Hot Springs, Arkansas. Later that year, she is diagnosed with kidney disease.

1917 Walker joins the board of the Circle for Negro War Relief to support black soldiers fighting in World War I.

1918 Walker's mansion, Villa Lewaro, is completed.

1919 Walker attempts in January to attend the Paris Peace Conference, but her passport is denied. In May, she dies at her home in New York.

GLOSSARY

Atlanta Compromise A speech by Booker T. Washington that said black people should not seek out political power in exchange for economic stability and learning trade skills.

Black Cabinet An informal group of black advisors that Mary McLeod Bethune brought together when she worked for the government.

buoy To support or to raise the spirits of.

civil rights movement A time when black people and white supporters worked to eliminate discrimination based on race and do away with Jim Crow laws.

consecrate To devote to a purpose with deep solemnity or dedication.

discrimination Unjust treatment of people based on their race, age, or sex.

entrepreneur A person who starts and operates a business, often taking on an above average risk.

Fifteenth Amendment An addition to the US Constitution that gave voting rights to all men no matter their race, color, or whether they were previously slaves.

Fourteenth Amendment An addition to the constitution that gave all people equal protection under the law.

Freedman's Bureau An organization created by Congress in 1865 to help former slaves and poor whites in the South after the Civil War.

good hair The idea that those with straighter, smoother hair and lighter skin were better.

hot comb A heated metal comb used to straighten and smooth curly hair.

incorporated business A business that legally becomes set apart from the people that founded the business.

Jim Crow laws Laws passed in the South after the Civil War to enforce segregation.

Ku Klux Klan A secret organization that started after the slaves were freed that uses violence and intimidation to restore white supremacy.

lynching A public execution committed by a mob to punish someone or to intimidate a group of people.

mission school A school started and run by a church or Christian missionaries.

NAACP National Association for the Advancement of Colored People; an organization that works to ensure civil rights and equality for all people.

natural hair When people of African descent keep their hair in its natural texture rather than straightening it.

permeate To spread or diffuse through something.

philanthropy Promoting the welfare of others, especially through donations to charity.

Plessy v. Ferguson A court case based on a mixed-race man, Homer Plessy, trying to ride a white rail car, which found Plessy guilty and validated the idea of "separate but equal."

puller A styling tool that pulled and stretched hair to make it straighter; an alternative to the hot comb.

pyramid selling Also called multilevel marketing; a strategy where products or services are sold by nonsalaried employees that are paid based on what they sell.

quintessential Something that is perfectly typical or representative of a kind of person or thing.

rapport A friendly connection to someone, especially with empathy or mutual understanding that makes communication easy.

Reconstruction A period of time when the US government tried to bring the South into the Union as quickly as possible; others wanted to give more rights to recently freed slaves.

rheumatism Several conditions that have inflamed or painful muscles, joints, or tissues, such as arthritis.

ringworm A fungal infection that can lead to bald patches on the scalp and bad rashes on other parts of the body.

sales agent Someone who sells products for a company and is paid based on what they sell.

segregation Keeping people of different races separate from each other in day-to-day life.

sharecropping When a landowner leases parts of their land to people who farm on it in exchange for a share of the crops.

surrogate A substitute or a replacement.

Talented Tenth A class of African American leaders in the early twentieth century; this term was made popular by W. E. B. Du Bois.

touring car An early automobile that had an open body and seats four or more people; these were popular in the early twentieth century before closed body cars became affordable.

tumultuous Marked by violent or a lot of turbulence or upheaval.

tycoon A businessperson who has tremendous wealth, power, and influence.

vocational training education that helps people develop the skills to work in a specific trade or craft.

Walker system A hygiene and beauty regimen that included cleaning and treating the scalp, brushing, applying a protective lotion, and using a hot comb.

white supremacist A belief that white people are better than people of other races and should dominate them.

SOURCES

INTRODUCTION

1. A'Lelia Bundles, *On Her Own Ground* (New York: Washington Square Press, 2001), 269.

CHAPTER ONE

1. Ayana D. Byrd and Lori L. Tharps, *Hair Story: Untangling the Roots of Black Hair in America, Revised Edition* (New York: St. Martin's Griffin, 2014), 20.

2. Eric Foner, "Why Reconstruction Matters," *New York Times*, March 28, 2015, https://www.nytimes.com/2015/03/29/opinion/sunday/why-reconstruction-matters.html.

3. Phil Edwards, "How Ida B. Wells Became a Trailblazing Journalist," *Vox*, July 16, 2015, https://www.vox.com/2015/7/16/8978257/ida-b-wells.

4. Melissa Block, "Here's What's Become of a Historic All-Black Town in the Mississippi Delta," *Public Radio*, March 8, 2017, https://www.npr.org/2017/03/08/515814287/heres-whats-become-of-a-historic-all-black-town-in-the-mississippi-delta.

5. Patricia Sullivan, *Lift Every Voice: The NAACP and the Making of the Civil Rights Movement* (New York: The New Press, 2009), 420.

6. Byrd and Tharps, *Hair Story*, 4.

CHAPTER TWO

1. Byrd and Tharps, *Hair Story*, 35.

2. Bundles, *On Her Own Ground*, 41.

3. Ibid., 48.

4. Henry Louis Gates, Jr., "Who Was the 1st Black Millionairess?" *The Root*, June 24, 2013, https://www.theroot.com/who-was-the-1st-black-millionairess-1790897002.

5. Bundles, *On Her Own Ground*, 136.

6. Ibid., 180.

7. Ibid., 216

8. Ibid., 200.

9. Ibid., 269.

10. Lagace, Martha, "HBS Cases: Beauty Entrepreneur Madam Walker," Harvard Business School, June 25, 2007, https://hbswk.hbs.edu/item/hbs-cases-beauty-entrepreneur-madam-walker.

CHAPTER THREE

1. Darlene Clark Hine, *Black Women in America,* 2nd edition, vol. 2 (New York: Oxford University Press, 2005), 320.

2. "Eleanor and Mary McLeod Bethune," PBS.org, American Experience, 2018, http://www.pbs.org/wgbh/americanexperience/features/eleanor-bethune.

3. Hine and Thompson, *A Shining Thread of Hope*, 252.

4. Bundles, *On Her Own Ground*, 277.

5. Booker T. Washington, "The Atlanta Compromise Speech," BlackPast.org, 2017, Accessed December 3, 2018, https://blackpast.org/1895-booker-t-washington-atlanta-compromise-speech.

6. Raymond W. Smock, *Booker T. Washington: Black Leadership in the Age of Jim Crow*, Chicago: Ivan R. Dee, 2009, 155.

7. W. E. B. Du Bois, "The Talented Tenth," Accessed December 3, 2018, https://glc.yale.edu/talented-tenth-excerpts.

CHAPTER FOUR

1. Byrd and Tharps, *Hair Story*, 34.

2. Bundles, *On Her Own Ground*, 212.

3. Ibid., 213.

4. Tyrone McKinley Freeman, "Gospel of Giving: The Philanthropy of Madam C.J. Walker, 1867–1919," Doctoral dissertation, Indiana University, 2014, 103.

5. Ibid., 209.

6. Bundles, *On Her Own Ground*, 126.

7. Ibid., 120.

8. Ibid., 179.

9. Freeman, "Gospel of Giving," 177.

CHAPTER FIVE

1. Byrd and Tharps, *Hair Story*, 13.

2. Freeman, "Gospel of Giving," 63.

3. Ibid., 96.

4. Ibid., 41–42.

5. Byrd and Tharps, *Hair Story*, 79.

6. Ibid., 78.

7. Freeman, "Gospel of Giving," 138.

8. Adam Coombs, "Entrepreneurial Uplift and the Making of a Black Modernity 1910–1937," Doctoral dissertation, Indiana University, 2017, 137.

9. Freeman, "Gospel of Giving," 155–156.

10. Davarian L. Baldwin, *Chicago's New Negroes: Modernity, the Great Migration, and Black Urban Life* (Chapel Hill, NC: The University of North Carolina Press, 2007), 70.

11. Coombs, "Entrepreneurial Uplift and the Making of a Black Modernity 1910–1937," 157.

12. Byrd and Tharps, *Hair Story*, 19.

13. Ibid, *Hair Story*, 35.

CHAPTER SIX

1. Michael Martin, "Black-Owned Beauty Shops Groom Political Activism." NPR.org, Tell Me More, December 28, 2011, https://www.npr.org/2011/12/28/144381812/black-owned-beauty-shops-groom-political-activism.

2. Bundles, *On Her Own Ground*, 151.

3. The Root Staff, "After More Than a Century, Madam C.J. Walker's Hair Products Are Back," *The Root*, March 2, 2016, https://www.theroot.com/after-more-than-a-century-madam-c-j-walker-s-hair-pro-1790854467.

4. Ibid.

FURTHER INFORMATION

BOOKS

Bundles, A'Lelia. *All About Madam C.J. Walker*. Indianapolis, IN: Blue River Press, 2017.

———. *Madam Walker Theatre Center: An Indianapolis Treasure*. Charleston, SC: Arcadia Publishing, 2013.

Byrd, Ayana D., and Lori L. Tharps. *Hair Story: Untangling the Roots of Black Hair in America*. New York: St. Martin's Press, 2014.

Fremon, David K. *The Jim Crow Laws and Racism*. New York: Enslow Publishing, 2015.

Krohn, Katherine, and Richard Dominquez. *Madam C.J. Walker and New Cosmetics.* North Mankato, MN: Capstone Press, 2006.

WEBSITES

BlackPast.org
https://www.blackpast.org

An online reference center for African American History, this nonprofit organization's site boasts fifteen thousand pages that features black public figures, speeches of black activists, historic places and subjects, and more.

Madam C.J. Walker
http://www.madamcjwalker.com

The official website of Madam C.J. Walker and her family, it provides articles and photos about Walker, her daughter Lelia, the company products, and more.

NAACP
https://www.naacp.org

One of Walker's favorite organizations, the NAACP is alive and well today. It has become a powerful force for equal rights, encouraging voter registration, and more.

MUSEUMS/ORGANIZATIONS

HairOnPurpose Conference
159 20th Street
Brooklyn, NY 11232

Madam Walker Theatre Center
History and Heritage Center
617 Indiana Avenue
Indianapolis, IN 46202

The Madam C.J. Walker Museum
54 Hilliard Street NE
Atlanta, GA 30312

National Museum of African American
History and Culture
1400 Constitution Avenue NW
Washington, DC 20560

National Women's Hall of Fame
76 Fall Street
Seneca Falls, NY 13148

BIBLIOGRAPHY

Baldwin, Davarian L. *Chicago's New Negroes: Modernity, the Great Migration, and Black Urban Life*. Chapel Hill, NC: The University of North Carolina Press, 2007.

Block, Melissa. "Here's What's Become of a Historic All-Black Town in the Mississippi Delta." National Public Radio. March 8, 2017. https://www.npr.org/2017/03/08/515814287/heres-whats-become-of-a-historic-all-black-town-in-the-mississippi-delta.

Biography.com Editors. "Booker T. Washington Biography." A&E Television Networks: Biography. March 1, 2018. https://www.biography.com/people/booker-t-washington-9524663.

Bundles, A'Lelia Perry. *On Her Own Ground: The Life and Times of Madam C.J. Walker*. New York: Scribner, 2001.

Byrd, Ayana D., and Lori L. Tharps. *Hair Story: Untangling the Roots of Black Hair in America*. New York: St. Martin's Griffin, 2014.

Chow, Andrew R. "Octavia Spencer to Star in 'Madam C.J. Walker' on Netflix." *New York Times*. July 30, 2018. https://www.nytimes.com/2018/07/30/arts/television/octavia-spencer-madam-cj-walker-netflix.html.

Conklin, Ben. "Ida B. Wells and Her Crusade for Racial Justice." Los Angeles, California: Constitutional Rights Foundation, 2018. http://www.crf-usa.org/images/pdf/Ida-B-Wells.pdf.

Coombs, Adam. "Entrepreneurial Uplift and the Making of a Black Modernity 1910-1937" PhD diss., Indiana University, 2017.

Driskell, Jay. "Making Waves: Beauty Salons and the Black Freedom Struggle." *American History*. November 3, 2016. http://americanhistory.si.edu/blog/making-waves-beauty-salons-and-black-freedom-struggle.

Edwards, June. *Women in American Education, 1820-1955: The Female Force and Educational Reform*. Connecticut: Greenwood Press, 2002. 112-121.

"Eleanor and Mary McLeod Bethune." PBS.org. American Experience, 2018. http://www.pbs.org/wgbh/americanexperience/features/eleanor-bethune.

Foner, Eric. "Why Reconstruction Matters." *New York Times*. March 28, 2015. https://www.nytimes.com/2015/03/29/opinion/sunday/why-reconstruction-matters.html.

France, Lisa Respers. "In the Black Culture, a Richness of Hairstory." CNN.com, July 20, 2009. http://www.cnn.com/2009/LIVING/06/24/bia.black.hair/index.html.

Fullam, Anne C. "New Stamp Honors Mme. C.J. Walker." *New York Times*. June 14, 1998. https://www.nytimes.

com/1998/06/14/nyregion/new-stamp-honors-mme-c-j-walker.html.

Freeman, Tyrone McKinley. "Gospel of Giving: The Philanthropy of Madam C.J. Walker, 1867–1919" PhD diss., Indiana University, 2014.

Gates, Jr., Henry Louis. "Who Was the 1st Black Millionairess?" *The Root*. June 24, 2013. https://www.theroot.com/who-was-the-1st-black-millionairess-1790897002.

Hansan, J.E. "Jim Crow Laws and Racial Segregation." Richmond, Virginia: Social Welfare History Project, 2011. https://socialwelfare.library.vcu.edu/eras/civil-war-reconstruction/jim-crow-laws-andracial-segregation.

Hine, Darlene Clark, ed. *Black Women in America*. Second edition, vol. 2. New York: Oxford University Press, 2005.

Hine, Darlene Clark, and Kathleen Thompson. *A Shining Thread of Hope: The History of Black Women in America*. New York: Broadway Books, 1988.

History.com Editors. "Andrew Carnegie." A&E Television Networks: History. August 21, 2018. https://www.history.com/topics/19th-century/andrew-carnegie.

———. "John D. Rockefeller." A&E Television Networks: History. September 19, 2018. https://www.history.com/topics/early-20th-century-us/john-d-rockefeller.

———. "*Plessy v. Ferguson.*" A&E Television Networks. August 21, 2018. https://www.history.com/topics/black-history/plessy-v-ferguson.

———. "Reconstruction." History, A&E Television Networks. August 29, 2018. https://www.history.com/topics/american-civil-war/reconstruction.

———. "W. E. B. Du Bois." A&E Television Networks: History. September 12, 2018. https://www.history.com/topics/black-history/w-e-b-du-bois.

IBJ Staff. "Madam Walker Theatre to get $15M Renovation, Operational Help." *Indianapolis Business Journal*, January 19, 2018. https://www.ibj.com/articles/67155-madame-walker-theatre-to-get-15m-renovation-operational-help.

Kansas Historical Society. "Benjamin 'Pap' Singleton." Accessed October 2, 2018. https://www.kshs.org/kansapedia/benjamin-pap-singleton/12205.

Lagace, Martha. "HBS Cases: Beauty Entrepreneur Madam Walker." Harvard Business School. June 25, 2007. https://hbswk.hbs.edu/item/hbs-cases-beauty-entrepreneur-madam-walker.

Martin, Michael. "Black-Owned Beauty Shops Groom Political Activism." NPR.org: Tell Me More. December 28, 2011. https://www.npr.org/2011/12/28/144381812/black-owned-beauty-shops-groom-political-activism.

Michals, Debra. "Madam C.J. Walker." National Women's History Museum. 2015. https://www.womenshistory.org/education-resources/biographies/madam-cj-walker.

———. "Mary McLeod Bethune." National Women's History Museum, 2015. https://www.womenshistory.org/education-resources/biographies/mary-mcleod-bethune.

"Obituary: Wealthiest Negress Dead." *New York Times*. May 26, 1919. https://archive.nytimes.com/www.nytimes.com/learning/general/onthisday/bday/1223.html.

Quintana, Maria L. "Malone, Annie Turnbo (1869–1957)." BlackPast.org. https://blackpast.org/aah/annie-turnbo-malone-1869-1957.

"The Rise & Fall of Jim Crow." Television. New York: Educational Broadcasting Corporation, 2002.

Ruffin II, Herbert G. "David Bend, Mississippi (1865–1887)." BlackPast.org. https://blackpast.org/aah/davis-bend-mississippi-1865-1887.

———. "Mound Bayou (1887–)." BlackPast.org. https://blackpast.org/aah/mound-bayou-1887.

Smock, Raymond W. "Booker T. Washington: Black Leadership in the Age of Jim Crow." Chicago, IL: Ivan R. Dee, 2009.

The Root Staff. "After More Than a Century, Madam C.J. Walker's Hair Products Are Back." *The Root*. March 2,

2016. https://www.theroot.com/after-more-than-a-century-madam-c-j-walker-s-hair-pro-1790854467.

Wada, Kayomi. "National Association of Colored Women's Clubs, Inc. (1896)." Accessed October 30, 2018. BlackPast.org. https://blackpast.org/aah/national-association-colored-women-s-clubs-inc-1896.

Washington, Booker T. "The Atlanta Compromise Speech." BlackPast.org. Accessed October 30, 2018. https://blackpast.org/1895-booker-t-washington-atlanta-compromise-speech.

Worthan, Robert A. *The Sociological Souls of Black Folk*. Lanham, MD: Lexington Books, 2011.

INDEX

Page numbers in **boldface** refer to images.

ABOUT THE AUTHOR

PJ Graham is an education writer and blogger. She worked for more than twenty years as a writer and editor for an education company and several newspapers, writing educational activity books and user guides as well as feature articles and entertainment reviews. Graham lives in southeast Kansas with her family and several pets. In her spare time, she enjoys hiking, photography, gardening, hand drumming, role-playing games, and travel.